TRICKS
AND GAMES
TO TEACH YOUR DOG

SOPHIE COLLINS
with **SUELLEN DAINTY**

ivy
Ivy Press

First published in the UK in 2012 by
Ivy Press
210 High Street
Lewes
East Sussex BN7 2NS
United Kingdom
www.ivypress.co.uk

British Library Cataloguing-in-Publication Data
A catalogue record for this book is available from the British Library

ISBN: 978-1-908005-69-4

Material in this book first appeared in *50 Games to Play With Your Dog* (2008)
and *50 Tricks to Teach Your Dog* (2011).

This book was conceived, designed and produced by
Ivy Press

Creative Director Peter Bridgewater
Publisher Susan Kelly
Art Director Wayne Blades
Senior Editor Jayne Ansell
Designer Ginny Zeal
Photographer Nick Ridley
Illustrator Joanna Kerr

This book has been published with the intent to provide accurate and authoritative
information in regard to the subject matter within. While every reasonable precaution
has been taken in preparation of this book, the author and publisher expressly disclaim
responsibility for any errors, omissions or adverse effects arising from the use or
application of the information contained herein. The techniques and suggestions are
used at the reader's discretion and are not to be considered a substitute for veterinary
care. If you suspect a medical problem consult your vet.

The author and publisher would like to thank the following for permission to
reproduce photographs: © A. Inden/zefa/Corbis, page 174; © Jupiter Images,
page 175 top; © Waltraud Ingerl/iStockphoto, page 176; © Lawrence Manning/
Corbis, page 177; © Getty Images, page 178; © Index Stock Imagery/Photolibrary,
page 179 top.

Printed in China
Colour Origination by Ivy Press Reprographics

9 8 7 6 5 4 3 2 1

TRICKS
AND GAMES
TO TEACH YOUR DOG

Contents

||||||||||||||||||||||||||||||||||||||||||||||||||||||||||||||||||||||||||||||||||||||||||||||||||||||||||||||||||||||||||||||||||||||||||

Introduction

How much does play matter to your dog? If he has good food, plenty of exercise and somewhere comfortable to rest during his downtime, do you really need to play with him, too? Or spend your own downtime teaching him tricks? Well, yes. Why? There's a whole host of arguments for teaching your pet lots of games and tricks, but here are just a few of them:

Dogs are one of the few species – humans are one of the others – to enjoy play as adults. There are social, practical reasons for this, as research suggests that dogs use play both to learn things and to get rid of stress. Dogs are clever – some very clever – and, just like people, they need to stretch their minds as well as their bodies to stay healthy and avoid boredom (and remember, a bored, bright dog may well be a dog that gets himself into mischief). As social mammals, dogs need plenty of interaction, too, whether that's with you, their honorary pack leader, or other dogs, and play is one of the most enjoyable ways to interact.

Teaching your pet reinforces your role as his leader, and will help to build the bond you already have together. If your dog is used to looking to you for his fun, then it should also be easier for you to catch and deflect his attention when he's thinking about something you don't want him to do – whether it's barking at the postman or bounding up over-enthusiastically to an unknown dog.

You can use games both to reinforce trust and to convince your dog that you're his best buddy. If your dog tends to act on his own initiative – sometimes a bit more than you'd like him to – then having fun with you can also lead him to look more naturally to you for guidance when an unfamiliar situation arises. Independent dogs are often the brightest (and they might be the ones who would manage best if they had to live in the wild), but they can also be the hardest to manage as domestic pets if they aren't given clear guidance.

Things to bear in mind: Start and finish every session, whether you're teaching a trick or playing a game, with something your dog is completely familiar with, so you ensure you always begin and end with good vibes. If your dog seems slow to pick things up, take your time and keep learning sessions short: dogs' learning rates are very, very variable. Teach little and often, and stay calm and upbeat. Never push your dog too hard; if he's looking frustrated or fed up, you've gone on for too long – and the most important thing of all is that you both have fun!

Keep it Safe

The tricks and games that follow include some options for every kind of dog: small, large, young, or old. Even if your beloved pet is elderly or hasn't spent much time learning new things, there'll still be some simple ideas you'll find that you can teach her. Do pay attention to the boxes on the pages – they offer safety advice when it's necessary and include other useful information and alternative suggestions for different elements for a game or trick to make it suitable for small or large breeds.

Pay attention to your dog when you're teaching active tricks. Usually, if a dog finds it physically uncomfortable to do a trick, she'll refuse to try it, so if she's normally eager to earn rewards and attention but is failing to engage with a particular game, it may not be the right one for her. Never assume that your pet is being obstinate if she doesn't appear to want to do something, and never coerce her physically; not only is this ineffective, it may have the very undesirable side effect of making her scared of you or even of playing in general.

Jumping, in particular, should be taught carefully. Puppies shouldn't strain their joints while they are still growing, and elderly dogs who have back problems or who are stiff in the hips shouldn't jump or try any game that involves 'crawling' on their bellies. Stick to some of the more mentally stimulating options if you have a dog who isn't very strong or agile physically.

And one last warning: work with objects that are safe for your dog to play with. Toys manufactured specifically for dogs are the best options for hunt- or bring-the-object games. If you have a very 'mouthy' dog who is strongly focused on mouthing and chewing any object that comes into her path, teach any collecting games with suitable props – nothing too small or that can be too easily chewed to pieces.

Once you have taken all the safety advice into consideration, you can stop worrying and play with your dog wholeheartedly. You'll be rewarded with an enthusiastic pet who is thoroughly enjoying her dedicated time with you.

Working With Your Dog

If you've never made a habit of dedicated play-and-training sessions with your dog, it's worth thinking about his individual qualities before you begin – working with his strengths will get you the best results in whatever it is that you're teaching him.

What does he like to do? Does he love running and jumping best? If so, maybe you should start with something that is agility based. Is he the thoughtful type? He may thrive on some of the tougher working-it-out choices. What behaviour do you want to encourage? It's surprising how many owners will teach their dog a game that involves jumping on the couch – and then complain when he jumps on the couch after the game is over. Be sure to play fair; only teach him things that you'll be happy for him to do when your play session is finished.

Think, too, about what your time together offers him. Almost every pet loves to spend time with his owner, but you should offer other payoffs, too. When he's starting to learn, if you find things going slowly, break a game or trick into plenty of steps and stages and reward even a tiny advance. Don't let the session go on for too long – five minutes at a time is plenty for a dog who's concentrating hard and trying to understand what it is that you want him to do. You don't want a turn to become boring; your pet must be enthusiastic about engaging with you and associate you with good things if you want to achieve positive results together.

Get used to encouraging him with your voice – and always use either an upbeat tone (for a dog who's heading in the right direction with the trick) or a low, calm 'Uh-uh' if he's getting it wrong and needs to think again. Make sure that you keep your voice as positive as your attitude – dogs are finely attuned to tone and some are particularly noise sensitive. Don't hector him, and if you find that you're feeling frustrated yourself, don't raise your voice. Instead, consider whether it's time for the pair of you to take a short break and sit down together with a snack!

YAWN!!!

Saying What You Mean

When trainers and behaviourists start to assess dogs alongside their owners, one of their most frequent findings is that owners aren't saying what they think they are – or at least, not as far as the dog's concerned! It's hard for humans to remember that, however many words dogs pick up and however good they are at interpreting human intentions, they don't speak English – and most humans don't speak dog or even read its basics very well.

Whole books have been written on the subject of 'reading' your dog and on telling her things in a language that she can understand (and they're worth hunting out if you have the time – some offer great insights) but here are a few basic tips that should help your pet to read what you're saying more clearly:

- Watch your body language. Are you moving involuntarily when you offer a verbal cue? One error owners frequently make without realising is to lean towards their pet when they're asking her to come to them. To a dog, this reads as a mixed signal – and if you're not careful, it could become one of many.

- Don't loom. You'll read this again in some of the following games, but it bears saying more than once. Give your dog her own body space; she doesn't like someone much bigger than her leaning over and encroaching into her body space any more than you would.

- Watch your tone. We've already mentioned keeping it upbeat, but remember, too, to match your voice to the instruction you're giving. Sl-o-o-w, long, low noises will calm things down; happy, upbeat sounds will speed things up.

- Only say it once. This is the hardest thing of all for a human to master. Give your dog the chance to learn what a verbal cue means. Don't repeat it in a lot of variations 'Come, come to me, good girl, that's it, COME HERE' sounds like a complicated configuration to a dog. If 'Come' doesn't bring her running, then at the least try to repeat only what you said before, without making it any more complicated than it was the first time.

- If you use visual signals and verbal cues, make sure they always complement one another – don't mix and match and assume your dog will understand.

Clicker Training

USING A CLICKER

Clicker training has become immensely popular over the last decade. Many trainers use the clicker for teaching tricks because it can reinforce the behaviour or action you want in your dog with very precise timing. The clicker is a small box with a metal tongue, which, when pressed with your thumb, makes a very clear 'click'. You first accustom your dog to listening for the click by clicking, then – immediately – giving him a treat. Once he's used to the idea that click equals treat, you can get specific with the behaviour you want.

The crucial part, though, is the timing – which has to be precise to a fraction of a second, or you may find you're rewarding your dog just as he's stopping what you want him to do. If you're interested in the idea of using a clicker, try to take a couple of classes or read up on it first; they're great for training, but they do have to be used correctly.

Refreshing the Basics

Chances are that if you have an adult dog, he's already familiar with these three basics. But it may be that both of you could do with a refresher course before you move on to more complex games or tricks – if so, practise the following for a minute or two at the start of every play session.

SIT

Stand in front of your dog with a treat in your hand. Raise your hand; as his nose goes up to follow the treat, he'll automatically lower his bottom. Take your hand slightly over his head and, as he goes into a sit, give him the verbal cue 'Sit' and give him the treat.

STAY

Put your dog in a sit, let him see that you're holding a treat, then back up a couple of paces, saying 'Stay' as you do. If he starts to get up, ask him to sit again and, once again, back up. At first give him the treat for even a couple of seconds of 'Stay'; as he gets used to it, you can try making him stay for slightly longer each time.

DOWN

Kneel facing your dog and ask him to sit. Holding a treat in your hand, slide it slowly forward in front of him, moving it a little farther as he leans forward to try to reach it. Say 'Down' as he moves downward; as soon as he's fully lying down, give him the treat.

Simple Tricks

Whatever your dog's age, size or intrinsic personality, you'll be able to teach him some of these little tricks. It's helpful if he already knows how to perform 'Sit', 'Down' and 'Stay'; if he's rusty on these (or if he's simply never learned), take a look back at page 15 for a speedy refresher course. If you've never tried to teach your dog to do anything specific before, you'll find it easiest to start with something he loves to do anyway, so take note of his everyday behaviour to see if he gives you any clues. Also, beginning with something simple means that he can enjoy some rapid success (and the treats and praise that go with it) and it will build his confidence for tougher options.

▶ **ONE** Most dogs will run immediately after a toy or ball that has been thrown. As your dog starts to run, say 'Fetch'. As she reaches her objective and picks the ball up, praise her.

Return to Sender

Some dog breeds, such as labradors and golden retrievers, seem to be born to play 'Fetch' games. Not every dog will be so keen, but 'Fetch' is a great way to double the amount of exercise your dog gets (while you simply stand and throw!), so it's worth persevering until your pet gets the idea. If she's slow to pick it up, keep the session short and move on to something else. Remember: never bore your pet when playing!

PLAYING 'FETCH' IN WATER

Dogs who like water and who enjoy 'Fetch' will probably be thrilled if you offer to combine the two. Play at the beach, or choose a quiet lake or pond, and throw carefully: don't disturb wildlife or swimmers. This is a great game for older dogs who may be stiffening up a little: swimming doesn't strain their joints.

SAFETY Make sure that what you throw is safe for your dog to fetch. If you live with a 'Fetch' enthusiast, invest in a ball of just the right size for her to pick up and a 'thrower' that will project it much further than would mere arm power. Small balls and toys or sticks are all classic examples, but they're not ideal for throwing; if a dog gets overexcited she can choke on too small a toy, and sticks can splinter in a dog's mouth if they are grabbed too energetically.

▲ TWO As soon as your dog picks up the ball, say to her 'Come'. As she turns to move towards you, encourage her enthusiastically. If your dog then wanders off at this point, start again from the initial throw so that she begins to get the idea of a sequence.

▶ THREE When your dog returns to you, give the 'Sit' instruction. As your dog sits she may naturally drop the ball, but if not, crouch down and offer her a treat in exchange. As soon as she drops the ball, praise her lavishly.

▶ **ONE** If you find that your dog is too excited to return the ball or toy you use for 'Fetch' games, collect two toys he is equally fond of before you start. Throw the first and let him rush off to collect it.

Play it Again

Some dogs love playing 'Fetch' so much that they become overexcited and refuse to give up the ball or toy that they've just retrieved. The easiest way to cure a dog of this habit while still keeping the game fun is to exchange objects with him. This also helps to stop him from becoming over-obsessed with a single toy, and to understand the principle of exchange; if he knows that giving something up to you makes even better things happen, he's unlikely to get too possessive of objects that he sees as 'his'. It will also help if he manages to get hold of something that he really shouldn't have, such as a shoe from your favourite pair. If he knows he's going to get something just as good in exchange, he'll be happy to give things up when asked.

USING 'DROP'

If your dog is reluctant to give up his toys, teach him the 'Drop' command. Place your hand gently under his jaw as he holds a ball in his mouth, then say 'Drop' and carefully take the ball from him. Then give the ball back as a reward, so your dog knows that he won't be deprived of his toy just because he obeyed you.

▲ TWO As your dog picks up the first toy, call to him to catch his attention and wave the second in the air. Most dogs will run towards you; some will instantly drop the toy they're holding in order to grab the new one. If your dog isn't one of them, see the box on the left.

▶ THREE As soon as your dog gives up the first toy, throw the second one for him. While he's collecting it, retrieve the original toy and, as he returns to you, repeat the sequence.

21

High Five

This repertoire basic is suitable for any size of dog and is usually simple to teach. If your dog is big, you can kneel in front of her and hold your hands at her natural paw level when you ask her to give you a 'High five'; with a smaller dog you can sit cross-legged and lower your hands a little. You can also practise a 'High five' from a standing position. Some dogs find it easier to start with a double-paw raise – technically, a 'High ten' – before balancing only one paw against your palm.

SAFETY When you're working with your pet face-to-face, remember that most dogs prefer not to make prolonged, direct eye contact, particularly with someone who's exactly at their eye level. A stare is rude and challenging in dog language, so don't stare at her as you teach this trick.

▶ ONE Ask your dog to sit down and, depending on her size, kneel or sit opposite her, or stand 30–60 cm (1–2 ft) in front of her, so that you're face-to-face.

◀ **TWO** Holding up one of your hands, say 'High five' in an enthusiastic tone. Some dogs, eager for contact, will immediately raise a paw to meet your hand; others will need a touch on their paw or may even need you to lift it up slightly to get the idea. It's usually easier to teach this trick using praise rather than food treats, because most dogs will go for treats directly with their mouths and it can slow down the association they make with lifting their paws.

▶ **THREE** As soon as your dog is pawing at your hand, place your outstretched palm flat against it, supporting it in position, and praise your dog the instant she's holding the pose. If you want to try a 'High ten', pat the other paw with your other hand, or, if your dog's happy to have her paws handled, pick it up and gently place it in position. The second that her paws are in place, praise her warmly, even if they're only there for an instant (you can build up to a slightly longer pose when she's got the idea). The dog here is shown in a begging 'High ten' pose, sitting back on her hindquarters. Some dogs find it easier to balance while holding their paws up from this position than from a straight sit; encourage your dog to take whichever pose seems to come most naturally.

ONE Look closely and you'll notice your dog tends to use either his left or his right side more often. All dogs favour one side; it will be the side he takes off from when starting to move. Use this side to teach him. Begin by asking him to go into a 'Sit'.

Shake a Paw

This game comes naturally to most dogs. They use pawing a great deal in play and between themselves, and they often develop an annoying habit of pawing 'their' humans when they want attention or a game. As well as being enjoyable for you to teach and your dog to learn, instructing your pet to shake a paw can help you to control pawing at other times when it's not welcome; by associating pawing with a specific command, your dog is less likely to do it unasked.

TWO Sit down in front of him and lightly touch the muscle of the shoulder of the paw you want him to lift. His front leg will lift slightly, automatically. He won't need much prompting for this one; pawing is a natural behaviour for dogs.

▼ **THREE** As his paw lifts, take it in your hand, shake it gently and say 'Shake a paw'. Use an underhand position; covering his paw with your hand can threaten a nervous dog. When he's more confident, you can ask him to do it when you're standing in front of him.

WAVE HELLO

||||||||||||||||||||||||||||||||||||||||||||

When your dog can shake hands on his own, you can extend the game by teaching him to wave. Stand back slightly as he holds out his paw. He will paw the air, and as he does so you can teach him the command 'Wave hello'.

Left Paw, Right Paw

Like 'Shake a paw' on the previous page, this is a useful trick if your dog needs reminders to watch her manners when she's trying to attract your attention. Teaching her to offer a specific paw for a 'High five' will be a useful distraction – and instead of annoying people, she'll charm them. You can use straightforward 'Left paw' and 'Right paw' cues to teach this one, but if you have a very 'nosy' dog, you may have to remind her that she should be raising a paw to your hand rather than using her nose. Most dogs have a preferred paw that they'll always use first, so be sure to alternate the 'right' and 'left' cues in various different sequences while you're teaching to ensure that she learns to use both sides.

▼ ONE Ask your dog to sit and, depending on her size, kneel or sit opposite her, or stand 30–60 cm (1–2 ft) in front of her, so that you're face to face. Using your right hand, tap her left foreleg, then raise your hand palm outwards, saying 'Left paw'. If necessary, pick her left paw up, holding it lightly in position against the palm of your right hand.

SHAKE HANDS
|||||||||||||||||||||||||||||||||||||||||||||||||||||||||

Some dogs find it much easier to lift their paws loosely than to hold a paw, pads out, to meet the palm of your hand. If you find a 'High five' hard to teach your dog, try teaching 'Shake a paw' (see pages 24–5), and add this to your dog's repertoire instead. You can come back to a 'High five' later, but always end a teaching session with something your dog already knows how to do – even if it's just a simple 'Sit' – to make sure that you finish on a positive note.

◀ **TWO** As soon as the paw is in the right place, praise your dog warmly. Don't worry if she doesn't hold the pose for more than a moment at first; as she becomes used to the trick, she'll be happy to stay in position for longer.

▶ **THREE** Repeat the sequence, but this time using your left hand and her right paw. Again, praise her as soon as she holds her right paw in the pose, even if it's just for an instant. If she doesn't get it right, simply say 'Uh-uh' and try again. Most dogs will quickly get the idea and, after a few sessions of practice, will enjoy playing a game of 'Left paw, right paw' as you run through a sequence of lefts and rights in rapid succession.

TWO   When he's sitting, take a treat and hold it above and slightly behind his nose, saying 'Say please' as you do so. He'll tilt his head back so he can see it while simultaneously reaching up to get it. As he leans backwards, his front paws will leave the floor and he'll balance back on his hindquarters.

ONE   'Say please' is easiest to teach with a food treat. Start by asking your dog to sit in front of you.

Say Please

This is the classic 'Beg' position, which you are probably familiar with from countless pictures of dogs. The begging pose comes very naturally to many smaller dogs; in general, though, the larger breeds are less enthusiastic about it and find it harder to balance upright on their hindquarters. If you have a big dog who's reluctant to beg, concentrate on a single-paw 'High five' instead – he'll find it easier to hold the position without becoming uncomfortable.

SAFETY It's an oft-quoted experts' rule that you shouldn't teach a long-backed or elderly dog to beg. While it's definitely not a good idea to impose the trick on an older dog or one that has back or hip problems, look out for what seems to come to your dog naturally. The little dachshund/spaniel cross shown in these pictures has a beautiful beg that is held very happily, despite having a long back. Usually, if your dog seems physically easy and happy with a position, it's safe for him to practise it.

▶ THREE As soon as he's balanced neatly, praise him and give him the treat. Don't ask him to hold the pose for more than a second or two at first, but as he becomes used to it, you can leave it a few moments longer before giving him the reward and releasing him.

Stand Up

This moves 'Say please' another step forwards – you ask your dog to stand on her hind legs and hold the pose for a moment or two. As with 'Say please', this trick is generally more popular with smaller dogs, who are likely to find it easier to do. It's a good trick to teach a dog that tends to stand on her hind legs and paw you when you don't want her to. By teaching her to respond to a signal in this way, she'll gradually become conditioned to take up the behaviour only when she hears the signal.

SAFETY It should go without saying that 'Stand up', like 'Say please', or any of the other games and tricks that call for a dog to spend some time balanced on only her back legs, aren't suitable to teach an old dog, or one that has any hip or back problems – it's too stressful for the joints and spine.

▶ ONE Ask your dog to sit down and stand facing her a little distance away.

◀ **TWO** When she's sitting comfortably, take a treat and hold it a little distance above and behind her nose. Her natural response will be to begin to pull her body up to reach the treat, as she would for 'Say please' on pages 28–9. As she rises up, say 'Stand up' in an encouraging voice and move the treat a little higher.

▶ **THREE** Instead of giving your dog the treat as she sinks back on her hindquarters, encourage her to stretch just a bit further (you could try an upbeat 'Hup' sound, too). As soon as she's standing completely on her back legs, give her the treat and praise her for her performance. Practise regularly until she can stand on her back legs easily without losing her balance.

▶ ONE To walk confidently, your dog needs to be happy standing on his back legs, so before starting this trick make sure that your pet is relaxed about standing upright. When he's in an easy stand, continue to face him, treat in hand, held slightly above his nose level, and with a step or two's distance between you.

Walk Along

When your small dog is relaxed and standing at your request, see if you can teach him to walk on his back legs, too. If he's good at this trick, he's conquered one of the basic moves of doggy dancing, so you can both feel proud of yourselves. You may even want to consider broadening his performance skills by adding spinning around and jumping on command to great walking and you've got the basics of a nice routine!

◀ **TWO** Begin to move very slowly backwards, increasing the distance between you slightly. As you do so, wave the treat and say 'Walk along'. If his balance is good enough, he'll take a step or two forwards to reach the treat. Give it to him and praise him as soon as he takes even a tiny, two-step 'walk'.

▶ **THREE** Gradually build the amount of time he can spend walking, leaving a second or so longer in each practice session before you give him the treat. Never continue to ask him to walk if he seems uncomfortable. Keep your practice sessions short and vary them with other kinds of games, so that he spends plenty of his time just running around on all fours!

Standing Ten

If a smaller dog isn't enthusiastic about performing a 'High five' when balanced on her hindquarters, but is happy with standing up and walking along on her hind legs, try teaching her a 'Standing ten' instead. Teach 'Stand up' (see pages 30–31) first, and don't try to extend it into a 'Standing ten' until she's balancing comfortably on her back legs. Because you'll be using both your hands, this trick is easier to teach without using food treats. Since you're holding out your hands to meet your dog's paws, you may want to kneel in front of her – it's a better position from which to place your hands flat against her pads and, if necessary, to support her and let her lean on you while she's still learning.

SAFETY Only use your hands to help your dog balance in this trick – avoid holding her up forcibly in position. Allow her to get down as soon as she wants to.

▼ TWO Ask her to 'Stand up', adding an enthusiastic 'Hup' sound if it helps her to get the message.

▶ ONE Kneel in front of your dog, facing her, leaving about 30 cm (1 ft) of space between you. Ask her to sit.

▼ **THREE** The moment that she's standing on her hind legs, hold out your hands, palms forward, and say 'Standing ten'. You can support her if she needs help in balancing, but try to get her paws placed pads out on your hands before she drops down again. Praise her warmly as soon as she's holding the pose, even if it's just for a second or two.

▲ ONE Start by asking your dog to get into a 'Down'. Then kneel beside him and hold out your hand as you would to give him a belly rub. He will happily roll down onto one side.

Rollover

Most dogs find 'Rollover' quite an easy command to obey, but before you start make sure that your dog is familiar with the 'Down' command: don't try to make him roll over unless he is. If he's confused about what you want, he won't enjoy trying to understand you, and you may damage his confidence in the things he already knows how to do. If you're using the clicker method to help your dog learn, you should only click and reward when your dog is beyond the point of no return in his rollover!

SAFETY Long-backed dogs, such as whippets and greyhounds, find rolling over more difficult than other more compact breeds. Don't persist if your dog looks uncomfortable.

◀ TWO Once your dog is lying on his side give him a brief belly rub, then produce a treat and, holding it over his ear, circle it slowly over his head. As you do so, say 'Rollover'. Some dogs find the movement very natural and will get the idea immediately, while with others it may take several tries. Reward your dog even if he hasn't managed a complete roll first time, then try again.

▼ THREE After a successful rollover, ask your dog to stand. When he's mastered a rollover confidently, try it without the treat, using just the circling hand signal, and treat him only on completion.

◀ ONE Get your dog's attention. As soon as she's focused on you, hold a treat above her nose and slowly begin to move your hand in a large circle a little above her head.

Spin Around

This trick acts as a building block towards a doggy dance routine – if that's what you'd both like to do! Your dog turns in a neat circle, following a circling motion of your hand and a verbal reminder. It can be taught entirely by using a treat as a lure, but don't forget to use the cue 'Spin around', too, or it may take longer for your dog to learn to take a spin without a food bribe. If she is one of many who spins naturally when she gets excited, you can reinforce the move by saying 'Spin around' and treating her whenever she starts to turn in a circle.

▲ TWO She'll follow your hand, and as she does so, say 'Spin around', continuing to move your hand around as you do so.

TEACHING TIP

When you're teaching your dog something completely new, don't stint on either treats or praise – plenty of both will help her to get the idea and keep her enthusiastic. As she learns more, praise her whenever she gets it right, but make the treats a bit more random – rewarding her every few successful attempts, but not every time. When you give food rewards, choose something she really loves; that way, she'll learn it's always worthwhile paying attention to you.

◀ THREE As she takes a full turn, praise your dog and, as she completes the spin, give her the treat.

▶ FOUR Repeat once or twice, encouraging your dog to turn the full circle before giving the treat, then try once or twice more, picking up speed and using the same cue but holding your finger out for your dog to follow rather than a treat. If you practise regularly, she'll soon be spinning in neat circles as soon as you ask her to.

Off to Bed

It's useful if your dog understands that sometimes he should settle down in his own space for a while. Most dogs will have a favourite quiet spot or two at home – places they'll go when they want some peace or a little downtime. If you want him out from underfoot, teach him that 'Off to bed' indicates that he should go somewhere specific. It helps, at least at first, if you use it only to refer to a single place or object (perhaps his basket or crate or his own towel or rug), rather than as a generic cue to sit down and stay quiet.

SEIZE THE MOMENT

||||||||||||||||||||||||||||||||||||||

This behaviour is easy to teach opportunistically – wait until your dog is on his way to lie down in 'his' spot, then tell him, as he sets off, 'Off to bed' and praise him when he lies down. This reinforces those times when he isn't so eager for a break but you want him to take one anyway!

▲ ONE Choose the place where you want your pet to go to bed with care. It should be somewhere he already likes to settle down. Wait until a time when he would usually be headed for a rest anyway – after a long walk or play session, perhaps, or when he's about to go off for an evening doze. Then indicate his space by looking towards it and say 'Off to bed'. If he looks at you for more clues, pat the blanket, basket, or whatever you are using and repeat the direction.

◀ **TWO** Few dogs need much more encouragement than this when they're already tired and ready for a break. Your dog will probably go over to his space and settle down right away.

◀ **THREE** If he's slow to head for 'his' place, walk over to it and call him over, then kneel down and encourage him to settle. As he lies down, praise and treat him, then leave him alone. After a few practice runs, he'll understand that 'Off to bed' means quiet time.

41

Learning a 'Stop' Signal

This trick will help you to get your dog to quieten down quickly when you need her to settle. An exuberant pet needs to learn that playtime stops when you say so. Your dog may find it hard to wind down after she's become worked up during a play session, so if you can learn to calm her down fast when you need to, it'll prove invaluable both at home and when you're out and about together. Remember that your tone of voice is very important in helping you to control your dog – use a happy, higher-pitched and upbeat tone when you want to raise your dog's levels of stimulation and a calm, quiet, level tone when you want to lower them. Never shout – it may be an effective way to catch her attention but it won't be helpful in getting her to obey you.

SMALL DOGS

No one wants a troublesome pet, but small dogs are often allowed to get away with more in terms of behaviour – purely because their size means they're less intrusive than bigger dogs when they act up. If you have a small dog, don't let her develop a Napoleon complex: teach her a 'Stop' sign (plus the 'Off to bed' cue) and you'll be helping to ensure she's welcome everywhere she goes.

▲ ONE Here's the situation: playtime is over, but your dog is still leaping around after her toy and ignoring you. If you try to take her toy away, she reads it as a sign that you're getting ready to play again. What should you do? Stay calm and stop chasing around after her. Instead, stand still and, using a low voice, say 'Stop' in an authoritative tone, at the same time holding out a hand tilted towards the floor.

▶ TWO If she ignores you, stay still and repeat 'Stop' in an even lower voice. It'll get through to her and she'll turn to you. As soon as you have her attention, ask her to do something she's completely familiar with ('Sit' is always a good choice here). She'll probably sit automatically, because the 'Stop' routine has calmed her down slightly and she's paying heed again. Praise her warmly as soon as she settles.

▶ THREE Repeat the sequence regularly, both when your dog is revved up and excited and when she's calmer. At first, you won't invariably get results when your dog is very excited, but if you practise it daily, you'll find that, gradually, she will begin to settle automatically when you ask her to 'Stop'. Ignore failed attempts, but praise successful ones lavishly.

43

Answer the Door

Most dogs love to answer the door, and sometimes their excited barking and jumping can be almost uncontrollable. If you teach your dog to bark on request when someone arrives at the door, however, you'll find that it's also easier to stop him from being noisy, because he's learned the barking as a behaviour he performs when you ask him to, rather than a reflex action that he does purely because he wants to.

▲ ONE If your dog already barks when someone comes to the door, look out for the exact moment at which he begins and, as he does so, tell him to 'Answer the door'. Speak in the upbeat tone you use for positive instruction; he'll be happy to continue to bark! If, on the other hand, you own one of the rare dogs that doesn't bark to alert you to visitors, you'll have to wait until he starts to bark in some other context, perhaps during an exciting game.

◀ **TWO** Once your dog is barking, run to the door with him (if he isn't already there), then stop the barking using your downward hand signal and a serious, low voiced 'Stop' as described on pages 42–3. It will take a little practice to get your dog barking on demand and stopping when you ask, but it's worth mastering because it means that you won't have a problem with constant, annoying barking at other times. Practise consistently and regularly – daily if you can.

▶ **THREE** Sometimes you'll find it works well to ask your dog to do something else as soon as he stops barking – this will distract him from starting again. Suggest something easy that he already knows – 'Sit' or 'Down' are good options.

Buried Treasure

A sandpit is enthusiastically welcomed into the play repertoire of many dogs. It's especially appealing to dogs that love to dig, such as most terrier breeds, and dogs that like to track scent will enjoy it too. The sandpit can also solve the problem of a dog that keeps digging up your flowerbeds: by giving her somewhere she can dig legitimately, you're allowing her to indulge her natural instincts in a suitable way. If your dog has ever been trained to use a litter tray, she may not be able to distinguish between it and a sandpit – so pick another game! Cover the sandpit when you're not out in the garden with your dog so that it doesn't become a magnet for the local cats, and the sand stays dry if there's a shower of rain.

▲ **ONE** Show your dog a favourite toy. As soon as you've got her attention, turn away, or (if you've started indoors) run outside to hide it in the sandpit.

▼ **TWO** The first time you bury a toy, leave a corner sticking out. Run with your dog to the sandpit, telling her to 'Find the toy'. If she doesn't jump in and dig it up right away, indicate where it is with your hand.

THE RIGHT SAND

||||||||||||||||||||||||||||||||||||||||||||||||||

Make sure you buy the fine sand that is used specifically for sandpits, not the coarser builder's sand. The latter can be very harsh and abrasive, and may scratch the skin of an over-enthusiastic digger.

◀ THREE Found it! Now that your dog understands, you can introduce extra objects and bury them deeper. When you've taught her the names of several objects (see 'Learn the name', pages 110–11), ask her to bring you a particular one.

SAFETY Your sandpit should be a dedicated doggy sandpit, not one that children use too. Just as you would for a child's sandpit, check it for splinters or protruding nails before your dog first uses it.

▶ FOUR When your dog brings you the object, ask her to 'Give' as usual, then return the object to her – although you may find that she wants it to be buried again right away!

Rainy Day Tricks

Your dog's bouncing with energy but it's raining too hard to take her out for a long walk, and you can't stand her theatrical canine sighing any more. What should you do? This chapter has some ideas to keep you both occupied and out of trouble, even when you have to stay indoors. Whether you pick the dog-friendly 'Tin of Treats', the crowd-pleasing 'Are You Ashamed of Yourself?' or even the hilarious bubble-chasing game, there'll be something here to keep you both happily occupied until the sun comes out again.

Tin of Treats

This is simple to set up and a lot of fun for your dog. Your pet needs to lift the tennis ball right out of the muffin tin holes because they are too deep to let the ball simply to be pushed to one side. It doesn't need much, if any, teaching and most pets will quickly grasp the idea; however, if your dog is slow to pick it up, show her how to play the game by lifting out one or two balls yourself to reveal the treats underneath. The only dogs it isn't suitable for are those who are more interested in playing ball than in treats – in which case, you may find that your dog races into another room with a tennis ball and tries to tempt you into something more energetic!

SMALL DOGS

Tennis balls may be too hefty for tiny toy breeds to lift. If your pet fits into this category, hunt out a tin with small holes (a mini-muffin tin will work well provided that the holes aren't too deep) and smaller, lighter balls. Even the teeniest chihuahua should be able to manage a table tennis ball.

◀ ONE Take a muffin tin and as many tennis balls (or other balls of equivalent size) as you can gather together. Put one of your dog's favourite treats in each of the holes in the muffin tin, then place a tennis ball over the treat.

TWO Put the tin on the floor and lift one of the balls briefly to show your dog the treat underneath. Then push the tin towards her and let her go. She may try to push the tennis balls aside at first, but she'll soon get the hang of picking them up.

THREE Once she's earned one or two treats by taking the balls out of the tin, she'll become eager in her search for more. And as she gets more accomplished in emptying the tin, you can try a round or two against the clock. Keep the treats small, though – you don't want her to pile on the weight. And don't forget to wash the tin thoroughly before your next baking project!

Shy Dog

This is a guaranteed crowd pleaser; no dog who has learned it successfully will ever be short of a treat. The easiest way to begin is to wait until your dog naturally assumes a lying position with his nose tucked down between his paws. You may have to help him along a little if he doesn't often take up this pose. Whichever technique you choose, never, ever force your dog into this or any other pose. The way to develop your relationship with your pet is to use the natural trust between you to coax or treat him to do what you want. Coercion will always be counter-productive: not only will your dog enjoy playing and learning with you less, but you also risk damaging his trust in you.

▶ **TWO** Take one of his front paws (you can ask him to 'Shake a paw', see pages 24–5, if he already knows that one), shake it, then place it gently across his other one.

▶ **THREE** Place your hands lightly behind his ears and position his head between his paws. Don't force him: if he's not relaxed about being handled like this, you'll have to wait for the 'Shy dog' position to happen naturally.

◀ **FOUR** Kneel down beside him, saying 'Shy dog' as you praise and reward his position. Some dogs are natural actors and will look coyly up at you from between their paws. Make sure he gets plenty of praise for his acting ability.

◀ **ONE** Put your dog into a 'Sit/ Stay' position, and make sure she watches while you put a treat under the mat. Put it just under the edge at first so that it's easy for her to get.

Are You Ashamed of Yourself?

This is an excellent trick for when you have company (and it's a great rainy day trick, because it can take a while to learn). Practise it until your pet is proficient before performing in front of visitors – it's certain to win a round of applause. Pick a rug or mat that's a good weight for her to push up with her nose – this might be light, such as a bath mat, or, for a large dog, something a little heavier, like the edge of a rug or carpet runner. She should be able to pucker up the edge easily.

◀ **TWO** In an excited tone, say 'Are you ashamed of yourself?' and tap the edge of the mat with your hand. She'll start to push her nose under to hunt out the treat, puckering up the mat as she does. As she gets her nose under the edge, praise her.

▲ **THREE** If she's too quick to grab the treat without getting into the position you want, keep your hand under the edge of the mat and hold the treat in it. Give it to her only when her nose is right under the edge. When she's reliably pushing her nose under the mat, try using the command without the treat. Practise regularly and she'll soon be getting into the right position on the command.

BIG DOGS

Some larger dogs are less comfortable putting their heads right down on the floor to do this trick. If so, put the treat under a rug or cushion placed on a chair instead – your dog may be happier to perform when training involves her practising a trick at face level.

Take It

This is a great building block to all kinds of tricks and games. You're teaching your dog to take something in his mouth – either from your hand or (usually at the next stage) to pick it up from the floor. It comes completely naturally to some dogs, while others take a little time to learn it. You'll find it easiest to practise with something your dog already loves to play with. You won't have too much trouble teaching a ball enthusiast to 'take' a tennis ball, for example. And suit the prop to the dog: retrieving types may enjoy taking a plushy toy; more 'chewy' breeds might prefer something harder, with more resistance to it.

▲ ONE Pick up a toy that you've already seen your dog carrying around. Put him in a 'Sit' position and hold it out to him, saying 'Take it'. Most dogs will automatically take the toy. Praise him as soon as he has it in his mouth (if you use a clicker, the exact moment that he takes it from you is the point for clicking). After a second or two, take it back from him and give him a treat. Don't give a treat if he drops it before you take it back, but don't ask him to hold it for too long at first.

◄ TWO When your dog has become used to taking a toy from your hand and holding it himself, try 'Take it' with the same toy lying nearby on the floor.

◀ **THREE** Keep it very near for the first few attempts, and look at the toy as you say the cue. Again, praise (and, if you're using a clicker, click) immediately when he picks it up – make sure that your timing is exact, so that he knows exactly what he's getting the praise for. Gradually, you can wait a moment or two longer to praise as he picks up the toy more easily. Once he's got the idea, use the instruction with different toys, so that your dog associates the cue with the action rather than the toy and gets used to picking up different things.

▼ **FOUR** When your dog is picking up various toys with ease, you can make the cue the starting point of a game – ask him to 'Take it', then run outside with him carrying the toy and play a game with him. It'll make him even more eager to do as you ask.

Dinner Time

What could be cuter than a dog who brings you her dinner bowl when she's hungry? The only prop you need is a bowl that's light enough for your dog to carry easily, plus a dog that knows the 'Take it' command and is also happy to bring things to you. As she gets more confident in bringing the bowl, you'll be able to ask your dog to take it to visitors, too – just suggest that they ask her if it's her dinner time yet.

▼ ONE This trick has two parts: first the dog needs to pick up her bowl and then she must come to you and hand it over. Start by getting her to pick it up. Place the bowl on the floor close to you and your dog, and ask her to 'Take it'. Praise her when she takes it and holds it in her mouth.

SAFETY Only use light, plastic bowls for this trick. Dogs don't usually like to pick up metal objects in their mouths and it's not sensible to ask a dog to run around with a ceramic bowl, so play it safe with the plastic option.

▲ **TWO** As soon as she's picking up the bowl enthusiastically, ask her to bring it to you. If she already knows a 'Fetch' command, use that; if not, get her attention and ask her to 'Fetch' or 'Bring it', using an enthusiastic voice and body language. Use a treat as a lure if you find it helpful.

▶ **THREE** When she brings the bowl to you, say 'Dinner time' and praise her warmly as you take it from her (or exchange it for a treat). If you practise regularly, your dog will gradually cut out the interim steps when she sees the bowl, and she'll learn to bring it straight to you when she hears the 'Dinner time' cue.

Lion Tamer

Choose a small, low piece of furniture with a non-slip surface for this trick. Your dog will leap onto it, then sit, neatly posed, in a 'Stay' position – like a lion perching on a stool in an old-fashioned circus. Very small breeds can even be encouraged to go into a begging position, rather than simply sitting. If your dog's an enthusiastic jumper, he'll learn this one easily. Make sure you choose a piece of furniture that he's allowed to treat as 'his'; you should be consistent about where your dog is allowed to sit, so don't let him do something as part of a trick or game that he isn't allowed to do normally.

SMALL DOGS

||||||||||||||||||||||||||||||||||||||||||||||

If you can train your small dog to stay standing on a stool or ottoman when he's jumped, you've made a great start to a grooming session, because he'll be at a convenient level for you to give him an overall brushing and combing. Use the 'Hup' command, give him a treat, then ask him to stay.

▶ ONE Place the stool or ottoman in a clear area on the floor so that your dog has plenty of jumping space. Pat the top with your hand and say 'Hup'. Most dogs will take the cue right away; if yours isn't sure, gently pick him up and place him in position once or twice, giving him a treat when he's in a pose.

◀ TWO Standing is the best position if you're planning a grooming session (see box, left). However, if you simply want your dog to pose nicely, wait until he's standing on the ottoman, then ask him to sit.

▶ THREE Ask your dog to stay for a moment or two, praise him, and then release him. Most dogs like to be high up – they can see what's going on around them better. If you place 'his' lion tamer's stool near a window, you may find that he elects to use it as a regular perch to sit and watch the world go by.

SAFETY Encourage your dog to jump onto only non-slip surfaces. Those covered in upholstery or fabric are fine, but a varnished or wooden surface isn't a good idea – his paws may not be able to find a grip and he may fall.

Hugs 'n' Kisses

You probably already have a tactile relationship with your dog (most owners do), and you may find that she already hugs and kisses you of her own accord. Even if she does, it's nice to be able to ask for a kiss from someone who you're sure will be happy to oblige! This also has the charm of being an extremely simple game, because it's taught purely by reinforcing what a dog does anyway. It's easier to teach small dogs, because you can introduce your pet to the idea when she's already sitting in your lap. If you want to play the game with a much bigger dog, sit down alongside her before starting, so that your faces are on the same level.

▶ ONE Make sure your dog is sitting squarely on your lap so that she doesn't lose her balance.

SAFETY Don't play this game with a dog that has back problems or one with a long spine, such as a basset hound or a dachshund.

◀ **TWO** Lift your dog's paws and gently place them on your shoulders while saying 'Hug'. You can also introduce a hand signal for 'Hug'; simply cross your hands over your chest and tap your shoulders. Praise her as she moves in closer.

▶ **THREE** When your dog moves to lick your face, say 'Kisses' and praise her enthusiastically. When you've finished playing, always give the command 'Down'. If your dog is easily excited, end the game if she starts to get too boisterous, before the kisses become nips!

▼ **ONE** Your dog can begin from either a standing or a sitting position, whichever comes naturally. Start by crouching down next to him and asking him to go into a 'Down'.

▼ **TWO** As soon as he's down, give him the command to 'Rollover'. But – here's the clever part – just as he reaches the halfway stage, lying on his side, ask him to 'Wait' and give him a treat. Once he's settled on his side, try the command 'Play dead'.

Play Dead

This fits more into the category of trick than game, but no one who has seen a dog successfully performing it and subsequently receiving the praise that is his due could doubt that he enjoys it very much indeed. Although this trick is not especially hard to teach, it involves sequenced behaviour, so you must ensure that your dog is familiar with both the 'Down' and the 'Rollover' commands before attempting it. And when he's playing dead successfully, don't expect your pet to stay in position for long when he hears the laughter and applause of an amused audience watching him perform!

▼ THREE Once he's got the idea – and it will certainly take a little practice – you'll eventually be able to drop the first two commands and he will simply flop to the ground when you say 'Play dead'. If you want (and you're not troubled by accusations of tastelessness), you can introduce the hand signal of pointing your trigger finger.

▶ ONE   The easiest way to teach this is to wait until your dog begins to stretch out her front legs naturally. As your dog extends her front paws, say 'Bow', then praise and reward her. She'll be surprised at first, but when you've caught her mid-stretch and rewarded her several times, she'll start to get the idea.

Take a Bow

Watch your dog just going about her daily affairs and you'll notice that she stretches out her body and 'bows' down over her front legs as part of her regular stretching routine, when waking from a nap or getting ready for some lively activity. If you're quick, you can catch your pet as she goes into a natural bow, give her the command and treat her as she completes it. Many dogs like the position so much that they'll pick up the command very quickly. If this doesn't come naturally to your dog, take her through the steps above; she'll soon get the idea. Bow to her as you give the command, and watch her bow politely back.

SAFETY This isn't a game for an ageing, arthritic dog or a dog with a bad back. If you haven't seen your elderly dog adopting this position naturally for a while, don't encourage her to do it just for fun.

▶ TWO Next time she starts to stretch, place a treat just in front of her paws. At the same time, hold her tummy up with one hand and give the command 'Bow'. Dogs usually pick this one up quickly, and soon she won't need the support and will be bowing when you ask her.

Chasing Bubbles

Less a trick than an activity, bubble chasing can be an effective way to use up a bit of excess canine energy on a rainy day. Dogs are often simply amazed by bubbles, and you'll love the surprised expression on your pet's face as he finally gets right up to his elusive prey – only to have it go 'pop' on the end of his nose. You can use a child's bubble-blowing set or even a wand with a strong soap mixture to blow the bubbles with. Start gently, blowing a small string of bubbles close to your dog; then, when you've caught his attention, try sending them around the room or blowing them in front of an electric fan to get him jumping around after them.

AIR FARE

|||||||||||||||||||||||||||||||||||||||||||

If your dog becomes a serious bubble enthusiast, you can indulge him by buying some of the commercial just-for-dogs bubble options – you can find bacon- or chicken-scented bubble mixes online or in large pet shops – plus machines that will even do the bubble blowing for you.

DON'T TRY AT HOME IF ...

This little trick isn't right for every dog. Small dogs with short legs may not be able to take the position easily or will find it uncomfortable, while some dogs have sensitive paws and hate to have them handled by anyone at all. If your pet fits into either of these categories, don't push the trick on her. Try either the 'High five' trick or 'Shake a paw' option instead – most dogs are less worried about giving you a paw than they are about you picking up and handling a paw without their personal say-so.

Cross My Paws

This elegant posture seems to come easily to some of the larger breeds – owners of greyhounds and labradors will often find them adopting the languid, cross-paw 'relaxing' pose naturally. If this is true of your dog, all you need to do is to praise and give her a treat when you see your dog settle down and cross her paws. If it isn't something your dog does of her own accord, she may need a little help.

▲ ONE Wait until your dog has settled down and is lying in a relaxed pose. This is a good trick to practise when she's already had some exercise; otherwise, you may find that she jumps at the chance of interacting with you and leaps up, ready to play, as soon as you pay some attention to her.

▶ **TWO** Kneel down beside her, gently take hold of one of her paws, and lay it over the other. As you do so, say 'Cross your paws' enthusiastically. The instant her paws are in the right position, praise the dog and give her a treat.

▼ **THREE** Sit back on your heels and see if she holds the position. If she unfolds her paws, place them back in the crossed position. If she stays still, you can reinforce the pose with a 'Good dog'. Some dogs may paw at you as you leave their paws crossed. If yours is one of them, you can convert the raised paw into a handshake to finish off the trick.

Under the Bridge

In 'Under the bridge', you're teaching your dog to crawl under the 'bridge' of your raised knees as you sit on the floor. This is easiest to teach if you lure your dog with his favourite food treat. Small dogs will find it easier than larger breeds (they have more space to go through!) but most medium-sized dogs will also be happy to make the moves if you have a really delicious lure to tempt them through. If your dog really is too big for the space under your knees, teach the alternative option (see box, below).

▼ **ONE** Sit on the floor with your knees raised, leaving a gap under your legs. Call your dog to you and ask him to sit at one side of you.

BIG DOGS

If you have a really big dog, he won't be able to fit under your knees for this trick. Instead, find a space that's big enough for him to wriggle through with a little effort, perhaps under a hurdle bar set at the right height. Lure him through, holding a treat on the other side of the bar.

TWO   Take a treat in the hand opposite to your dog and hold your hand down at floor level on the opposite side from your dog. He'll lower his head and sniff at the treat; as he does, pull it slightly further away from the bridge made by your raised knees. Your dog will follow the treat through; say 'Through' as he does. As soon as he goes completely through the gap, give him the treat and praise him.

THREE   After a few tries, when your dog's following the lure with ease, try the trick again, but treat your dog only every second or third successful attempt. Don't stint on the verbal praise, though. After a little more practice, you'll find that you can fold your hands out of the way, and your dog will go under the bridge on just the 'Through' command.

Commando Crawl

If you've already taught your dog to go 'Under the bridge' (see pages 72–3), then she'll have some idea of the crawling action this sneaky-looking move calls for. She will need to be lying down but in the ready-to-go position before you start – if she's in a relaxed 'Down' with both her legs under her but to one side, she won't be in a good pose for crawling. It's best, too, to teach this trick on a soft, carpeted surface; most dogs will be happier to crawl on a surface that isn't too slippery or chilly.

▼ ONE Ask your dog to lie down, but start on the trick while she's still in an alert position – that is, before she switches into a completely relaxed position with her hindquarters lying over on one side. Have two or three food treats in your hand – you'll probably need more than one to encourage your dog to get a good crawl motion.

▼ TWO Hold a food treat a short distance from the ground, between finger and thumb, just out of your dog's reach. If he starts to get up, say 'Uh-uh' and ask him to lie down again.

▼ **THREE** Gradually move the treat away from her nose, keeping it at the same height from the floor (if you hold it at floor level, she'll try to push her nose under your hand to get the treat; if it's slightly raised from the floor, you'll be encouraging the crawl more effectively). As she creeps forwards, praise her effusively and give her the treat.

SAFETY Don't teach this trick to an elderly dog, one with a very long back, or one who has any history of back or hip trouble – the creeping movement may aggravate an existing problem.

▼ **FOUR** Put another treat in your hand and lure your dog forwards again. Stay aware of the height the treat is at, and the position it's luring your dog into. As she crawls just a little more, reward her again. This is a difficult pose for a dog to hold, so plentiful rewards and brief practice sessions are best. Don't go on too long; you don't want to strain her joints.

Back Up

This is one of those useful commands that can stop your pet in his tracks when he's making a nuisance of himself. When you're teaching 'Back up', remain very aware of your own body language and tone of voice. It's important to relay the message in your manner as well as in the verbal cue you're offering.

▶ ONE There's a time and a place for everything, so if your dog is leaping about energetically and paying no attention to you, here's a way to calm him down.

MIND YOUR LANGUAGE!

When you're calming your dog down and trying to focus him on you, use an authoritative tone and, when it's appropriate, a clear hand signal. Stand well back and don't loom into his body space, particularly if he is a small dog, because he may find this threatening and that won't help him to concentrate on what you want him to do.

▶ **TWO** Hold up your hand, using the signal shown, and say 'Back up' in a clear, calm voice. Say it just once; if you time it right, speaking into a quiet moment, your dog will stop what he's doing and turn his attention on you. Move towards him slightly as you speak.

◀ **THREE** Take advantage of the moment he's still to refocus him on something you want him to do. Maybe you'd like him to lie down and concentrate on a Kong toy full of treats for a while? Or play a quieter game of rolling a ball about, rather than jumping around the room. Whatever it is, make your move quickly, offering him the distraction. Remember: just as with children, it's always more successful to encourage something you *do* want them to do, rather than to concentrate solely on stopping a behaviour you don't like.

Squeak, Piggy, Squeak

Dogs are usually really enthusiastic about squeaky toys. 'Squeak, Piggy, Squeak' is the perfect game when it's raining hard outside and you have a houseful of people and a bored, underexercised dog on your hands. Several people together may enjoy this one, too, as your pet rushes from room to room eagerly seeking out the source of the noise. Try it with a variety of toys that make different noises – pet shops offer toys with a range of sounds, from a honking 'duck' call to a high-pitched squeak like a mouse.

◀ **ONE** One 'player' attracts your dog's attention with a squeaky toy. Everyone else who's playing takes a toy and hides in a different room around the house. You can conceal yourself behind the furniture or even in a cupboard if you want to increase the challenge for your dog. Then 'squeak' your toys in unison, while the person with the dog tells her to 'Go find'.

◀ **TWO** The first time you play, you may find that your dog needs leading to the first person in the sequence so that you can 'find' him or her together. After that, your dog will probably be eager to set off on her own.

▶ **THREE** As she finds each new player, that person should congratulate and pet her, and hand over the toy, if she wants it – though he may be too eager to get to the next person to want it just then. Encourage her to keep going until all the toys and people have been 'found'.

Just the
Two of You

You and your dog already love spending time together, and this section concentrates on some tricks and games that will enhance your closeness. They call on him to pay close attention to what you're teaching him, and you and your possessions act as props to the trick in many of them. Whether you want to walk arm-in-arm with your dog (a game that you'll want to encourage in only large breeds!) or to teach your pet to carry your bag or collect your keys before you go out together, you'll learn how to here. Plus you can find out how to teach your dog to hunt for you or chase you – both are good games for dogs that can seem a little too independent-minded for their own good!

Take My Arm

Just as 'Answer the door' can be a good tool in teaching an eager barker to bark only on demand, 'Take my arm' can be helpful in teaching your large dog that he should jump up only when invited. If you teach him to balance on your arm, too, it may curb his enthusiasm for jumping higher in order to smother your face with kisses. A dog who loves to take your arm can also be encouraged to 'Take a walk' – walking along a few paces with you, arm in, or rather on, arm.

◀ ONE Ask your dog to sit, and then place yourself standing slightly sideways to him. Hold the forearm nearest to him at a right angle and pat it with your other hand, saying 'Take my arm' as you do. This trick is probably easiest to teach without treats; you need him to focus on balancing his front legs rather than going for something with his mouth. If he hesitates to jump, make a small, encouraging 'Hup' noise.

SMALL DOGS

This isn't a trick for a small dog, even if he's an enthusiastic jumper. You can teach a variation to small breeds if you kneel or sit alongside them, with your arm angled in the same way. Don't be surprised, however, if a dog who loves to jump suddenly vaults high enough to give you a sloppy kiss when you're in such tempting proximity.

◀ **TWO** As soon as he makes the jump, use your forearm to steady him and help him to balance. Hold your arm in the way that seems easiest for him to grip with his paws, and praise him as soon as he's in the right position. Unless he's obviously happy standing in the pose, don't ask him to stay too long at first. With a few practice sessions, he'll soon be able to hold your arm for several seconds at a time.

Catch the Owner

While any game that encourages your dog to run away from you is a bad idea, enticing your dog to chase you as you run away from *her* is a great way to show her that she's the one who has to keep up with you, not the other way around. Both this and 'Come find' on pages 90–91 are useful if your dog's attention is prone to wander away from you. If you can make every time she comes to you into an enjoyable game, you're far more likely to be successful in the future when you're calling her away from something she wants to carry on doing. Plus it's good exercise for you, too.

▲ ONE This is best played outside – you won't be able to get far enough away from your dog indoors to start a chase. Wait until your dog is paying attention to something else and is already a little distance from you. Don't try it for the first time when she's doing something distracting (such as playing with her best dog friend) – eventually, you'll be able to get her to chase after you every time, but it will take some practice.

TEACHING TIP

If you can't run fast enough to give your dog a stimulating chase, enlist a friend to stand some distance away and take turns calling her to you. Most dogs will love racing between two people, getting praise and attention from both.

▶ TWO Start to run in the opposite direction from your dog. As you run, call to her in an excited voice, making plenty of upbeat noise – you can add whistling and hand claps if you want to. You can look over your shoulder to see if she's coming, but don't stop – keep running as fast as you can.

▼ THREE Dogs love to chase: as soon as she notices that you're initiating a game that she's more used to playing with other dogs, she'll eagerly race after you. Praise and make a fuss of her when she catches up – then run away again. Without the advantage of surprise, she's bound to catch up with you faster the second time around!

Walk Around

This is a development from spinning in a circle (see pages 38–9), but instead of chasing his tail, your dog does his turn with you in the centre of the turning ring instead. This is a popular doggy dancing staple; if you find that your pet's an eager performer, you could practise turning circles together to music – he's likely to be particularly enthusiastic if he feels that you're joining in, too. If your dog can follow a mark, try this trick without treats by asking him to follow your finger; however, if not, it's easy to teach using small food treats as a lure.

▲ ONE Begin by calling your dog to you: first get his attention, then, either holding a treat between two fingers or using a downward finger as a mark for him, begin to trace a circle around the front of your body, saying 'Walk around' as you start.

TWO As he begins to follow, take your hand around the side of your body. Keep the hand with the treat in it close to your legs so that the circle he is being brought in is neat and tight.

THREE Bring your hand as far behind your legs as you can, then quickly either switch the treat to your other hand (so you don't have to turn around yourself) or, if you're pointing, swap the hand you use to point with.

FOUR Wait until he's walked the full circle, then praise him and give him a treat.

87

▲ ONE Stand still with your legs shoulder-width apart. Hold a treat ready in your left hand. Your dog needs to be on your left side. Lure her to the front of your left leg and encourage her through your legs by switching the treat to your right hand. Now lure her around your right leg.

Walk 'n' Weave

This game suits an active dog that loves a challenge. It's perhaps not surprising that many of the masters of 'Walk 'n' weave' and 'Doggy dancing' in the show ring are border collies, a breed that is famous for its smartness and agility. This game isn't for every dog, but most breeds can master it, provided that you're consistent and patient while your pet is learning, and you don't persist in a session if your dog is getting bored. You should add it to your repertoire only when your dog has learned a number of other games and commands, and is used to working attentively with you.

▲ THREE Ready to walk 'n' weave? This one takes practice, so try it on your own first before trying to teach your dog. When she's on your left, lift your right leg. Don't forget your hand signals to lure her through! As your right foot hits the ground, lift your left leg and encourage her to weave around to your left side. Once you've both understood this move correctly, try walking slowly forwards.

▲ TWO At first, give the command 'Weave', or use a clicker, but as your dog learns the game you can drop the command – and the treats – and use hand signals only. You'll need to lean down at first to reward her, but as you both progress you'll find you can stand up straighter and she'll still follow your movements easily.

TAKE YOUR TIME

This is a game for which you need a good existing rapport with your dog; it's not one for novices or puppies. Keep the sessions short, expect her to take a little time to learn, and don't let your dog get bored or confused. If you can both master this game, you've learned one of the basic moves for doggy dancing!

Come Find

Like 'Catch the owner' (see pages 84–5), this is a good game to play if your dog seems inclined to take your constant presence for granted. It's easiest to play outside (which offers a larger, more unfamiliar space and more things that you can hide behind) but when the weather's bad you can try it indoors instead. Swap the places you hide around and don't rule out the really unexpected; in fact, apply the same rules as you would playing with people – your dog will be amazed and thrilled to finally locate you in a wardrobe, for instance! And it's good training for your dog to learn that it's worth keeping an eye out for you, whatever other distractions are going on.

(see pages 84–5)

TEACHING TIP

You can usually play this game only once every day or two, because after one round your dog will stay by your side, waiting for the next thing to happen. However, it's a good way to start off a training session, because he'll end it in an attentive mindset, ready to learn something new.

▶ ONE Wait until your dog is slightly distracted (only slightly – five minutes after you've presented him with a new marrow bone is not the moment to try this game), then hide from him. Ideally, pick somewhere unexpected, at least a couple of rooms away; don't make it too easy.

► **TWO** Call your dog to you, or whistle, or even use the click of a clicker. Your dog will be alert and start looking for you. If he's taking longer than expected, make the noise again, but don't keep calling him – remember, it's his job to track you down, and he's already got the built-in advantage of a sharp sense of smell.

► **THREE** When he eventually finds you – in the cupboard, behind the couch, under a table – make a big fuss of him.

Follow the Target

It's useful to teach your dog to mark a target with her nose, because her ability to do this can be the building block to more complex tricks – for example, you can use this to teach her to close a door for herself. This exercise is simple and shows you how to teach your dog to 'follow' your hand or finger with her nose. The aim is to get her to 'mark' your hand with her nose.

▼ ONE Ask your dog to sit down in front of you. Stand or kneel in front of her, put a small treat between the base of two of the fingers of your right hand, then hold it out to her, palm outward. Say 'Target' as you do so.

BIG AND SMALL DOGS

With a big dog, teach 'Follow the target' from a standing position, but keep your hand down low at the level of her nose and ask her to sit, as you would a smaller breed, before you start. With a tiny or toy dog, get right down to her level, sitting on the ground, to get your hand level with her nose, and also ensure that she sits before you start.

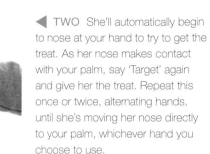

◀ **TWO** She'll automatically begin to nose at your hand to try to get the treat. As her nose makes contact with your palm, say 'Target' again and give her the treat. Repeat this once or twice, alternating hands, until she's moving her nose directly to your palm, whichever hand you choose to use.

◀ **THREE** When she's got the idea, hold your hand out to her, palm out, but without a treat between the fingers, using 'Target' as the cue again. When she touches your hand with her nose, give her a treat, but from the other hand. After a few repeats, only give her a treat once every two or three times she gets it right. When she's invariably marking your palm, try giving a visual cue by holding out a single finger – eventually, she'll be able to 'mark' this, too.

ONE

Stand to one side of your dog, so that you're both facing the same way. Ask him to sit down alongside you. You may find that you (or your dog) are naturally right- or left-sided; pick whichever side is most comfortable for you both. Have a handful of small treats ready.

Look Left, Look Right and Cross the Road

This is a cute trick for when you're out and about together – plenty of dogs have learned to sit obediently at the curb until you tell them it's time to cross, but far fewer have learned to check the traffic flow by looking left and right in the same way that you do. You'll raise a laugh from other pedestrians when your dog shows off his savvy before you cross together. Make sure that he's getting it perfect every time before you show it off to strangers.

TEACHING TIP

Although it can be tempting to practise this trick while keeping your dog on the lead (after all, he'll be restrained when you're out and about), it's better if he learns it off the lead. You want him to follow what you say rather than 'help' him with the movements of the lead; it's best for you to rely on your voice to direct him.

TWO Say 'Look left', at the same time holding a treat well off on his left-hand side. He'll turn his head, and as he does so, praise him and give him a treat. Repeat on the other side, saying 'Look right', and holding the treat well off to his right side. Again, he'll turn to look at it; again, praise him and give him a treat as he does. Repeat this several times, alternating sides. As soon as he's clearly associating the head turn with the verbal cue, cut down the treats, offering one only every second or third successful attempt.

THREE Now that he's looking left and right, it's time to 'Cross the road'. Go through steps one and two, then walk forwards, saying 'And ... cross the road' enthusiastically as you do. Practise the whole sequence over several sessions until he's cue perfect, then take him out to show off in public how smart he is.

▶ **ONE** Wait until it's nearly time to go out and your dog is getting excited about her forthcoming walk. Put the lead in a place where it's easily accessible to her (on the floor, or on a low chair or table), then get her attention, indicate the lead, and ask her to 'Take it'.

Walk Yourself

Many dogs love to hold something in their mouths when they're out for a walk – and you can teach your dog to carry her lead when you're not holding the other end of it. A woven fabric or tape lead is the best kind to use for this; it's easier for her to pick up and carry than the heavier chain or thick leather kind. It's best to teach the 'Take it' instruction on pages 56–7 before you start on 'Walk yourself', and also to practise this around the house and garden before you ask her to carry her lead on a walk; you want to be sure that she's not prone to drop it before you go out.

▶ TWO Praise her when she picks it up. If it's trailing and she seems to be finding it awkward to carry, knot it up a little to make it easier for her. Now ask her to 'Come along' and walk briskly away. She'll probably follow you, and if you don't take the lead she's likely to keep carrying it. If she drops it, ask her to 'Take it' again and wait until she picks it up before walking on.

▼ THREE After a few sessions, you should be able to ask her to carry her lead whenever you're out in a place where it's safe for her to do so. Make sure she understands that when she's 'Walking herself', she's also accompanying you – when it's time for off-the-lead play, reclaim the lead so it doesn't get lost.

Carry My Bag

If your dog has learned to carry his lead, you can try extending the trick and asking him to take one of your bags for you. Pick a soft, washable bag – a fabric tote is ideal for larger breeds, but you may have to find something much smaller if you have a little dog. It's a good idea to put one or two light items in it before you start (you could include a packet of treats or a favourite toy for rewarding him after he's been carrying the bag for a while). Knot the handles if it will make it easier for your pet to carry.

◀ **ONE** As with 'Walk yourself' on pages 96–7, start by placing the bag somewhere accessible and obvious. Stand at the other end of the room and ask your dog to 'Take it'. If your dog starts to rummage about with the contents, however, discourage him with a firm 'Uh-uh'. As soon as he picks it up, praise him and call him to you.

◀ TWO He may be rather tentative about carrying something with some weight. If he hesitates or puts the bag down, ask him to 'Take it' again, and call him to you right away.

◀ THREE As soon as he gets it into his head that he needs to come to you with the bag, he's got the basic idea of the trick. Even if he's only carried it across the room, make a big fuss of him and look in the bag for a toy or a treat to reward him. Then practise regularly, increasing the distance between you. When your dog can bring you the bag from another room in the house, you can try the trick when out shopping. You can even ask him to hold your bag while you're getting out your purse to pay!

▲ ONE Stand with your back to your dog, and attract her attention by bending down and making smooching noises to her. Hold a treat down between your knees so that she can see it.

Peekaboo

In this trick, your dog walks between your legs from behind, then sits down, peeping out from between your knees. A dog will only place herself in this vulnerable position with someone she really trusts, so unless she's one of those rare pets who adores everyone she meets, don't expect her to perform this trick with anyone but you. This is a good choice if you have a natural performer; she'll look so cute peering out that she's certain to get a lot of laughter and praise from onlookers.

SMALL DOGS

A very small dog may hesitate before walking between your legs like this – if she seems nervous, try to make it less intimidating for her by kneeling instead, so that you're closer to her level, then lure her through with a treat just as you would if you were standing.

◀ **TWO** As soon as she's positioned directly behind you, pull your hand forwards to encourage her to walk between your legs, saying 'Peekaboo' as you do.

▶ **THREE** As she reaches the mid-point, ask her to sit, then praise her and give her a treat as soon as she does. Encourage her to sit for a few seconds before getting up again.

Fetch My Keys

Because a bunch of keys is small, hard and metallic, it is usually harder to succeed in getting your dog to pick it up than it would be something softer and easier on the mouth – so it's best to try 'Fetch my keys' after you've already taught your pet to 'Take' some more obviously appealing objects. Try attaching a small treat bag containing one or two tiny edibles to your keyring; it'll make the keys immediately more attractive to him.

SAFETY you have a young, excitable and naturally 'mouthy' dog, this may not be the best trick to teach him. You don't want him swallowing your car keys by accident! Use your common sense to decide whether this is a suitable trick for him.

▼ ONE Make sure that your dog watches you while you attach a small bag of treats to your keyring. Ask him to stand back while you place it on the floor. Then ask him to 'Fetch it'.

▲ TWO As he picks it up, call him to you, saying 'Fetch my keys'. Use an excited voice; you don't want to give him too long to think about whether he's going to get the treats out by himself or bring the keys to you.

▼ THREE As he brings the keys, keep calling him and encouraging him – as soon as he reaches you, take the keys, praise him lavishly, and give him a treat. Practise this trick in between fetching easier things, so that he becomes accustomed to bringing you a range of different items.

Treat Trail

Most dogs will happily – and quickly – find a food treat if you hide one and indicate in its general direction; their sense of smell is strong enough to take them there. Little pieces of cooked chicken, sausage or cheese are all perfect for this game, which is simply a pre-organised treasure hunt for the committed canine foodie. As always, be consistent with what you expect of your dog; if she's not allowed on the furniture, don't hide treats on the sofa. Pick a room in which you're happy to have her freely roaming and nosing around.

▲ ONE Get your dog used to the idea of finding the treat by letting her sniff it, then toss it away, just a little distance. Keep her on a lead if necessary, then let her go, saying 'Find it'. Then let her watch you place a treat somewhere she needs to nose it out – behind a flowerpot, perhaps, or in a storage box. Repeat 'Find it' as she sniffs it out.

◀▲ TWO In the course of a few play sessions, get your dog used to waiting while you hide two or three treats before asking her to find them. Now the fun really begins. While she sits and stays outside a room, hide half-a-dozen treats in various places. Then let your dog into the room and excitedly tell her to 'Find it'.

THREE She may be confused at first. She's smelling a lot of treats at once, and she hasn't watched them being hidden, so help her on her way by leading her to the first treat. Let her do all the 'finding' (actually nosing it out from where it's hidden) herself.

FOUR Once she's got the idea, you can hide treats in more challenging locations, extend the hunt across more than one room, or even take the Treat Trail outdoors.

Mind
Games

How smart is your dog? He's your beloved pet, so you've always believed he's super intelligent, but have you ever tested him? The games and tricks in this section will encourage him to think for himself and to try to figure out what it is that you want him to do, too. Some will need to be learned in several stages, while others can be long-term projects – for example, there's no reason why, if he can learn the names for four items, he shouldn't go on to learn the names for a dozen or more. Now that you've worked your way through the basics, it's time to stretch him a little …

1, 2, 3, Treat!

There's an order to everything – and the trick here is to lay out some treats and ask your dog to collect them, working from the topmost of three steps down to the lowest one. A hungry dog may gobble up all the snacks before she's got the idea, so use small treats and have a few 'Uh-uh' noises ready to let your dog know that she's not quite got it yet. If you teach this when she's already had a good run around, you may find that she's more able to focus.

TEACHING TIP

However hard you try, if you find that your dog gobbles down the treats without thinking about any 'trick' element, change things around a little. Teach her to 'Follow the target' (see pages 92–3) using your finger, then move your hand down the stairs, corner to corner, asking your dog to 'target' at each stop. If she's focused on you (and rewarded when she's successful at doing what you ask), she may find it easier to pick up.

◀ ONE Lay out half a dozen treats down the lowest steps of a flight of stairs: one in both top corners of each step. Bring your dog to the stairs, point to the top step, indicating the treat on one side, and ask her to 'Take it'. She won't need to be asked twice. Now indicate the second side of the step, and, as she eats the second treat, point to the third, on the step below.

SAFETY

Don't ask a dog with back trouble to do this trick – backing down the stairs won't be good for her joints. Instead, lay out half a dozen treats on flat surfaces in a sequence, so that she can learn to take them in order, but without climbing up or down any steps.

◀ **TWO** She'll need to back down to the second step to get the second section of treats. Again, indicate the two different sides for her. Then encourage her to take the last treats offered.

▼ **THREE** As she gets the idea, you'll find that you'll be able to run to the stairs with her and dash through the treat sequence quickly. Eventually, she'll be picking them up for herself, in order, without any pauses, and in double-quick time.

Learn the Name

Your pet probably already understands a range of words – very few dogs don't recognise 'dinner', 'walk' and 'bedtime', and many have far more words in their repertoire. The record is held by a border collie living in Germany that can identify well over 300 objects by name and, most impressively of all, can recognise them in pictures as well as in three-dimensional reality. Don't aim too high at first: start by teaching your dog two toys by name and asking him to pick up the one you indicate. Make sure he knows the 'Take it' cue (see pages 56–7) before starting on 'Learn the name'.

TEACHING TIP

If your dog is used to a clicker, it's particularly helpful with 'Learn the name' and 'Fetch the …' (see pages 112–13) because you can click at the exact point at which he starts to go for the right toy and reinforce his decision – it's faster and more precise than a verbal reinforcement.

▼ **ONE** Lay two familiar toys side by side on the floor. Don't start this game with a new toy – your dog may be too excited by the novelty of something fresh to play with to be able to concentrate on what you want him to do. Bring him into the room, walk over to the toys together and say 'Take your tugger' (or ball, Frisbee, etc) in an upbeat voice.

▶ **TWO** Your dog will probably recognise the 'Take ...' from 'Take it' – and he'll want to pick up a toy because there's a chance of starting a game with you. If he goes straight for the toy you named, praise him and give him a treat right away. If he makes the other choice, say 'Uh-uh' and indicate the right one. Again, as soon as he takes it, praise him and give him a treat. Repeat a few times until he's going straight for the toy you name and picking it up.

▶ **THREE** Now repeat the whole process, but this time naming the second toy: 'Take your ball'. He may get the idea right away, but if not, say 'Uh-uh' when he makes the wrong choice. If he makes the wrong choice again and begins to get frustrated, hand him the right toy, repeating 'Take your ball' as you do, then praise him as soon as he has it in his mouth. Practise daily, varying which toy you name, and how often, until he always selects the right one of the two.

Fetch the ...

When your dog is confident playing 'Learn the name', extend her repertoire by adding different objects to her lineup. Most pets are able to learn up to a dozen different objects, provided that you stay patient and cheerful while you're teaching and you practise regularly. When she understands that she's being asked to make a selection (and this can be a surprisingly difficult concept for even smart dogs to grasp), then you can also try adding one unfamiliar object to the lineup and asking her to 'Take the ...', simply using its unfamiliar name. Your dog may be able to deduce that you must be naming the unfamiliar object, because she knows the other names, and may also then select it to bring you. First things first, though: here's how to start to enlarge her vocabulary.

ONE Lay some toys on the floor. Pick two that you know your dog can already identify, and two that you haven't yet taught her. Start by asking her to 'Take' one of the familiar ones. When she gets it right, praise her and give her a treat.

◀ **TWO** Now follow up by asking her to 'Take' the other familiar toy. Again, when she gets it right, make a fuss of her. Then ask her to 'Take' one of the unfamiliar options; if she looks baffled, show her the toy you named and offer it to her, repeating 'Take your …' as you do. Step back and repeat, asking her to choose only the selected new option for several tries. When she's getting it right every time, go back to include the original two options, and alternate all three.

▶ **THREE** From this point, once your dog has learned three different toys, you can use the same method to add additional words and a bigger lineup of options. Always make sure that she's learned one thoroughly, though, before moving on to the next – and if she gets confused or frustrated, don't hesitate to go back to the beginning, reducing her options and asking her for an object that you know she's familiar with, to help build her confidence.

▼ TWO He'll probably walk through the cones happily, but he may not immediately grasp the turn around each cone to make the complete figure-of-eight. Hold your hand/treat quite low and guide him clearly as he takes the turn after passing through the cones.

▲ ONE Arrange two small, light cones as shown (you can buy these in large sports or pet shops). If your dog is happy to follow a finger, use that as his guide; if he needs a bit more incentive, use a treat as a lure for the first few tries. Hold up the finger or treat alongside the first cone and say 'Wind around'.

Wind Around

If your pet is a natural 'spinner' – that's a dog who loves to run in circles and chase his tail when he's excited – you'll probably find that he's a natural for weaving routines. This is a mini version of the weaving trial on a real agility course. If he turns out to like walking a figure-of-eight shape, you can add a few more mini cones to extend his options – although you may have to move outdoors to extend his 'course'!

BIG AND SMALL DOGS

||||||||||||||||||||||||||||||||||||||||||||||||||||||||||||||||

Suit the distance between the cones to the size of your dog; the bigger the dog, the more space he'll need for his turns. As he becomes confident in his turns, you can move the cones slightly closer together to make the 'weave' a little tougher.

▲ THREE Continue to guide him back through the gap and around the other cone. Repeat 'Wind around' if you need to, and if he doesn't seem to get the idea right away, you can walk just ahead of him and take the turns yourself, too.

▶ FOUR As he completes the figure-of-eight, praise him and give him a treat. Take another couple of turns. Eventually, he should be happy to make the turns on only a verbal cue.

Cone Ball

This game is a variation of a simple 'Fetch'. It will appeal strongly to any dog who is a ball enthusiast. When she's learned the basic version, you can place two or three cones, each topped by a tennis ball, in the garden and ask her to bring you one before you play a 'Fetch' game with her. That way, she'll get plenty of exercise. See if she can identify which ball to fetch if you point to the cone you want – some dogs seem to recognise the intention of 'their' humans pointing with a finger, while others appear completely baffled by it!

SMALL DOGS

|||||||||||||||||||||||||||||||||||||||||||||

If your dog is too little to reach a ball on even the smallest cone, improvise. You can balance a ball on an upturned plastic bowl, or any other accessible object. Don't ask a tiny dog to jump for 'Cone Ball' – the cone isn't stable enough for her to brace herself on.

▼ ONE Set up a small, light cone with a tennis ball balanced on top of it. (If your dog is magnetically drawn to any tennis ball she sees, it's best to do this out of sight.) Call her to you and ask her to 'Fetch the ball'. If she doesn't seem to get the idea immediately, run over to the cone with her and indicate the ball with your hand.

◀ **TWO** As she moves to pick the ball up from the cone, praise her. As soon as she has it in her mouth, call her to you, making a lot of enthusiastic noise.

▶ **THREE** When she reaches you, hold out your hand and ask her to give you the ball. If she's not immediately willing to give it up, take it from her mouth (gently – don't encourage her to think that you're playing tug with her). If she loves 'Fetch' games, throw it for her as a reward.

117 ||||||||||||

ACHOO!!!

▲ ONE Place a tissue box on a low, stable surface. Pull a tissue halfway out of it, and practise by saying 'Take it. Achoo!' while showing it to your dog. When he's happy to pull a tissue from the box (and this is probably the hardest part of the trick, so practise patiently until he's got it out), back off a step or two and repeat 'Take it. Achoo!' Your dog will take the cue to collect the tissue.

Caught a Cold

This is a great trick to show off when you have company. Cued by a loud, theatrical sneeze, your dog will run off to collect you a tissue from the box handily situated on a low surface nearby and run back to you with it firmly held in his mouth. True, it's likely to be a bit damp and squishy by the time it's 'handed' to you, but no matter, this is so sweet that it always wins a big round of applause. Practise it until he gets it perfect every time before you show off to your friends. Learn the trick stage by stage; it's quite complex, so be prepared for short, frequent sessions while you're teaching it.

TEACHING TIP

Some dogs seem to steady the tissue box with a paw naturally. However, if your pet knocks the box over and finds it hard to angle, use duct tape to stick it to the surface you've placed it on; he'll find it easier if all he has to do is focus on pulling out the tissue.

◀ **TWO** Praise him enthusiastically as he heads for the tissue box. At this point, he may be ready to pull the tissue out on his own, or he may need some help with a verbal cue.

▶ **THREE** Make sure that the tissue is pulled out of the box to the point where it's very easy for him to remove it. Give him plenty of encouragement as he pulls. As soon as he's got it free of the box, call him back to you.

◀ **FOUR** When he brings the tissue over, praise him lavishly and take the tissue (if he's reluctant to let it go, you can keep a treat concealed in your hand and engineer a neat swap with him).

ONE Make a parcel using several layers of thick paper and a prize in the centre – a dog treat or a squeaky toy should be enough incentive for her to play. Show it to her – wave it around a little if you need to attract her interest, then tear through one layer at a corner of the package and hand it to her.

TWO Encourage her to tear through a layer of paper and pull the smaller parcel out. Try not to let her tear right through at the first attempt (see box, right), or it will be a very short game. Just as she reaches the second layer, take the gift gently from her, saying 'Give me' as you do. Praise her warmly as soon as she gives it up to you.

Pass the Parcel

Any dog can unwrap a parcel if she can sniff a tasty treat inside, but what about if there are several layers? It takes a bright dog to learn how to undo one layer, hand the parcel back to you, and then take it back again for her next turn. Teach this trick with plenty of rewards along the way, or the sad, downcast expression of your dog as she hands back a parcel that she knows has something delicious inside may discourage you from practising until she has it perfect.

▶ THREE Let her watch as you tear a layer of paper off the parcel yourself, then hand it back to her, saying 'Go ahead'.

▼ FOUR You might not manage more than one handover the first few times you play this game; your dog will get so excited that she'll tear to the centre the second time you hand her the package. Try to control her excitement with your tone of voice – low and quiet – when you're giving the verbal cues; with time, she'll learn enough restraint to cope with two or three handovers before she goes for the prize.

TEACHING TIP

||||||||||||||||||||||||||||||||||||||||||||||

We wrapped the parcel in plenty of varied and colourful wrapping paper to show the layers clearly for the photography. However, you don't have to use special paper for your own version – your dog won't care if it's plain brown paper and layers of newspaper, as long as she's enjoying the game! Either wrap in thick layers or use heavy paper to ensure that she doesn't just tear straight through to the treat the moment she starts to use her teeth.

How Many Fingers?

Can your dog really count? Probably not, but you can make it look as if he can by asking him to bark the number of fingers you're holding up. Timing is absolutely crucial for this trick – you need to let him know not only exactly when to start barking but also just when to stop. And it's demanding for him, because he must learn from both verbal and visual signals (eventually, you'll be dropping the verbal ones). Be patient – unless your dog is one of the few who is really averse to barking, he'll get it in the end. The more fingers you start by holding up, the more time you're giving yourself to get him to stop on cue.

▼ **ONE** If your dog already barks on demand (for example, see 'Answer the door' on pages 44–5), then you can use this to start the 'counting'. If not, encourage him to bark with an exciting noise, using the verbal cue 'Count' and holding up one hand with the fingers spread out. It may take a while to teach, but don't move on to the second step until he is barking on cue to the verbal and visual signal.

▼ **TWO** Now teach him to stop the barking. As he begins, keep your hand held up for a moment or two, but after three or four barks use your other hand to give a 'stop' signal (hand down and palm in), saying 'Stop' in a low, calm voice as you do. Again, he'll eventually get the idea with plenty of practice. Be ready to praise him and give him a treat as soon as he stops.

▶ **THREE** As your dog becomes used to the visual cues, you can gradually abandon the verbal ones until he is barking and stopping purely on hand signals. Practise holding up four fingers, say, on your 'barking' hand, and stopping him barking exactly after four barks. Try a short practice every day until you both have your timings accurate – eventually you'll be able to reduce the number of fingers first to three and then two, increasing the number of options for him to bark his 'answers'.

Mark It

An untrained pet, shown a box with a treat in it, will usually use both paws and mouth to try to open the box to get at the treat. In 'Mark it', you're showing her how to lightly mark the box with her paw – as soon as she gets it right, she'll be given the treat as a reward. You'll need a small, light container with a tight-fitting lid and a really good food treat for this game. Cut a small hole or slit in the top of the container before you start so that your pet can smell the delicious morsel of sausage or cheese you've hidden inside.

▲ ONE Show your pet the box and let her sniff around it before you put any food inside. Then put the treat in while she isn't watching, close the lid, place it on the floor and call her in. She'll go straight for the box and start to sniff at it.

▼ **TWO** As soon as she's worked out that the treat is closed inside, she'll try to use both her mouth and paws to get the lid off. Don't let her do this for more than a second or two; instead, quickly step in, take one of her front paws and tap it lightly on the box, saying 'Mark it' as you do. If you use a clicker to teach, the exact moment that her paw touches the box lid is the time to click. Sit back, repeat 'Mark it' and see if she's made the connection between paw and cue. You may need to repeat it a few times before she understands that it's the paw movement that you want from her.

▶ **THREE** The moment she places a paw on the box of her own accord, take the lid off the box and give her the treat. At first you may need to reward an attempt – say, a paw movement towards the box. However, as she becomes used to the game, aim for a clear paw tap every time before you treat her.

Show Me

In 'Mark it', you taught your dog to show you where the treat is by putting his paw on the container; in this follow-up, you're going to ask him to choose from three options. As he already knows the cue that gets him the treat, adding to the number of boxes shouldn't hold him up for long, although he'll probably have to give them all a thorough sniff before making his selection. When he's used to playing, try some variants by putting treats in every box (he'll wonder which to mark first) or in two out of the three containers you've lined up. Offering him an unexpected option (and the possibility of an extra treat or two) will keep him enthusiastic about the game.

▼ **ONE** Start by laying out three lidded containers of about the same size, each with a small slit cut in the top. Put a treat in one box, bring your dog in, and ask him to 'Mark it'. He may have to sniff all three, but he'll readily identify which box has the treat in and mark it with his paw. Praise him and give him a treat – but now make things more complex.

▶ **TWO** Put tiny treats in two boxes and a larger one in the third. Line them up, call your dog in and ask him to 'Mark it' – which does he pick? Open whichever box he marks, give him what's inside, then ask him to mark another. When you've been through all three boxes, repeat the sequence and see if he goes for the big treat first.

▼ **THREE** Try playing favourites – different kinds of treats in each box. Can he pick out his favourite? This game is fun for you because you're kept guessing about your dog's choices, and it's fun for him because it puts him in a no-lose situation – whichever container he goes for, there's at least one treat to be had.

Night, Night

This is another quite demanding trick. If your dog masters it she'll have every right to feel very pleased with herself, because it has several different steps. She'll need to be familiar and comfortable with the 'Play dead' game (see pages 64–5) before you start. As always with the harder tricks and games you're learning with your dog, keep your teaching sessions short, fun and positive, and play some of the easier games in between. If your dog has a favourite cloth or blanket that she enjoys mouthing, incorporate it into the game, as she'll be used to moving it with her teeth.

▲ **ONE** Get your dog used to being covered with a blanket before you start teaching in earnest. Some dogs don't like being covered up, so it may take some time and patience before she feels comfortable. Then tell your dog to 'Play dead', and, when she's lying down on her side, cover her with her blanket.

▲ **TWO** Saying 'Night, night', offer her a corner of her blanket, or place it gently in her mouth. Don't be discouraged if she jumps up. Just go back to the beginning. Only try this a few times, though, before moving on to something else. When she eventually takes her blanket, praise and treat her.

▼ **THREE** When she's learned to grab her blanket, you'll eventually be able to bypass the 'Play dead' command and just say 'Night, night'.

The Hard Stuff

You and your pet have worked through a few tricks together, so now it's time for the hard stuff. Of course, there have already been some options that called on the two of you to practise a lot in the previous sections, but this chapter offers a range of challenging extras. Follow the rules to ensure that your dog still has fun: make sure you're consistent when you teach, keep the lessons short and upbeat, and always, always stop or change things around if he's getting bored or frustrated by a game. An interested dog is a happy dog – and it's your job to ensure he stays engaged with you while he's learning.

Touch the Spot

Identifying and 'marking' a target wherever it's placed is a great start to some advanced learning (it's the main building block to teaching your dog to direct her strength and can be used to teach her to open a door, for example – see pages 136–7). Dogs vary on which part of them they choose to 'mark' with – one dog may prefer to use her nose, another her paw. Concentrate on asking her to mark or push the target with her paw, because it will carry more of her body weight behind it when you want to direct her strength to a specific task.

▲ ONE Take a plastic target (it's a round, plastic disc; you can buy them in pet shops, or use the plastic top from a tube of tennis balls or potato crisps) and a blob of poster putty. Start by sticking the target somewhere easy and accessible – you could just lay it on the floor. Then call your dog.

SAFETY Always place the target on a stable surface for your pet; if she jumps to mark it and whatever you've secured it to slips and slithers about, she may become reluctant to touch it again.

▶ **TWO** Point to the target. As she goes to investigate, wait to see if she touches it with her nose or paw. If you use a clicker, click the second her paw touches the target, saying 'Touch' and give her a treat. Otherwise, wait for the right moment, but say 'Touch' and give her a treat in the same way. If she doesn't immediately make the connection, you can sit alongside the target and tap it with your finger or even gently place her paw on it, then give her the chance to do it for herself and praise her as soon as she gets it right.

▼ **THREE** As soon as she's regularly going straight for the target, move it around onto some different surfaces, such as a wall, a piece of furniture or even a person. She'll soon understand that, wherever the target is placed, 'Touch' is asking her to touch it with a paw.

Shut the Door

▲ ONE Before you start 'Shut the door', make sure that your pet has completely mastered 'Touch the spot' (see pages 132–3). When he's confidently touching the target every time, place it at his natural paw height on a closed door (something like a kitchen cabinet is ideal) and ask him to touch it.

You're settled on the sofa watching television when someone comes into the room and forgets to shut the door. How impressive if you can call to your dog and ask him to close the door for you! And your dog will love the laughter and praise when he does it successfully in front of company. Practise it thoroughly before you show it off, and when you're sure he'll do it when asked, keep your tone casual ('Casey, could you shut the door?') so that onlookers are even more surprised when he trots over on cue and pushes it closed.

SAFETY While your dog is learning this trick, it's best to hold the door yourself to make sure that it closes in a controlled way and doesn't fly shut, causing him to lose his balance. Even when he's learned it, ask him to shut only familiar doors that won't slam shut or be too heavy for him to push.

◀ TWO When you've practised a few times, move the target up, little by little, until he's standing and pushing the target at a height at which most of his body weight will be placed against the door.

▶ THREE Finally, ask him to 'Touch' a target placed high on a door that is slightly ajar. Hold it at the top so that it will close slowly as he pushes. Practise on one or two familiar doors, leaving them a little more open every time, and start to add 'Shut the door' as he jumps and pushes. Eventually, when he's used to jumping, pushing and balancing in a single sequence, you'll be able to remove the target altogether and ask him to 'Shut the door' for himself. Be generous with rewards while he's still learning; this is quite a tough trick, so you'll need to keep him motivated.

If you're teaching your dog to open doors, make sure that she won't come across anything dangerous with her newfound ability. Don't forget that lots of everyday household cleaning materials, for example, can be harmful to dogs, so if you teach her to open a cupboard, only that cupboard door should have a tug on it, and only safe treats or toys should be kept inside.

Open the Door

Just as impressive as 'Shut the door', this trick is usually considerably easier to teach. Dogs can't get a grip on most door handles, but if you tie a tug to the handle you want your dog to open, she'll get the idea quickly. Eventually, she may even be able to let herself out into the garden – but don't forget to teach her to close the door after herself!

▲ **ONE** Before you start, play a game of tug-of-war with your dog. Ideally, play with the rope or fabric you'll eventually be tying to the door handle so that your pet associates it with pulling (and games). When you play with her, say 'Pull' as she tugs at her end to help her connect the action with the word. After the game, loop the rope around handle of the door you want her to open and hand it to her, saying 'Pull'.

◀ **TWO** If she hesitates to take it in her mouth, pull on it a little yourself until she shows some interest, and then offer it to her again.

▼ **THREE** Once she has it in her mouth, she'll start to pull. As she pulls, keep a hand on top of the door so that it doesn't fly open and scare her. When the door starts to open, say 'Open the door' and give her praise and a treat. Gradually, as she becomes more confident, you'll be able to drop the 'Pull' cue and eventually simply send her to 'Open the door' by herself.

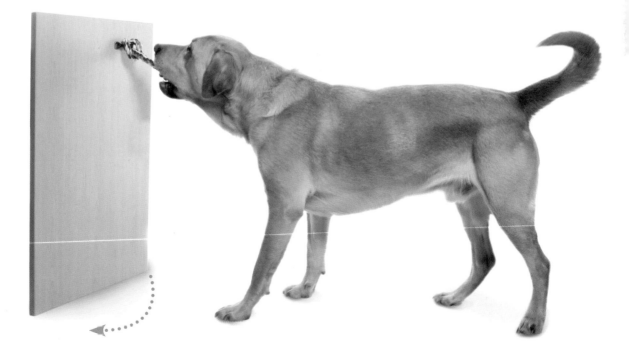

▼ ONE To 'fetch his snack' effectively, your pet needs first to have learned the steps to 'Open the door' on pages 136–7. When he confidently opens the door every time without needing your help, prepare a treat for him (make it something that you know he really loves and that will take a little time to eat) and place it inside the cupboard.

SMALL DOGS

||||||||||||||||||||||||||||||||||||||||||

This trick will work just as well for small dogs, but make sure the door he's expected to open to get to the snack isn't too heavy for him, and that the treat inside is portable once he has. A light cabinet door with a tug pull at a reachable level and a treat on the floor inside will work best for a little dog.

Fetch Your Snack

When you've taught your dog to open a cupboard door, it's great if he finds something worthwhile inside. This is a good party piece – you can wait until your guests are settling down for a meal around your table, then send your pet to collect his own snack so that you can all eat together. Something like an appropriately sized stuffed Nylabone toy will be a worthwhile snack for your dog to collect.

▼ TWO Accompany him to the cupboard and ask him to 'Open the door'. When he's opened it, point to the rawhide chew, stuffed Nylabone, or whatever other delicacy you've laid in an accessible place inside and say 'Fetch your snack'. He won't usually need much encouragement, but make sure it's placed so that he can reach it easily and pick it up in his mouth. If he seems uncertain whether he can just take it, repeat 'Fetch your snack' enthusiastically, picking it up and handing it to him at the same time.

▼ THREE If you practise regularly, your dog will gradually learn 'Fetch your snack' as a cue of its own, and you'll be able to dispense with the 'Open the door' cue. If you'd like a little regular downtime with your dog, you could even turn 'Fetch your snack' into a daily ritual, factoring in ten minutes' peace and quiet for you while he enjoys his treat.

► ONE Start the game by familiarising your dog with what's expected of her. Send a family member into another room and then say, 'Where's John?' As you do so, have John call her from another room, and treat her when she runs next door to greet John. When she's confidently finding John whether she's called or not, it's time to give her a letter to deliver. Hand her the letter, saying 'Where's John?' again.

Direct Delivery

This game will teach your dog to deliver notes, letters or small objects to anyone in the house. Keep the things he has to deliver easy for him to carry, and start with just one person's name. When, and only when, your dog has gone through the sequence above, you can start introducing other people into the mix. Eventually – and with lots of practice – you'll have converted your pet into an in-house mail carrier who can deliver the post to each family member, wherever he or she is in the house.

NO CHEWING

Retrieving breeds tend to carry things gently: it's bred into them. Other groups, though, such as terriers or toy breeds, may find it hard not to chew and mouth whatever they're given to carry. You may find it necessary, therefore, to add a 'no chewing' command to these dogs' repertoires.

▲ TWO As soon as the letter is safely held in your dog's mouth, have John call again from another room. At first your dog may drop the letter and rush to answer the call. If she does, pick it up and remind her to take it with her. Hand it to her again, saying 'Wait ...', then 'Where's John?'

◀ THREE As your dog arrives, get John to kneel down, hold out his hand and say 'Give'. As soon as the dog hands over the letter, John should treat her and give her lots of praise. This is a relatively complex sequence to teach, so you may have a few false starts before your pet is successful. Be patient and keep the training session short.

141

Catch the Treat

This is a hard trick for dogs to learn. Take it slowly, teach it in its component parts as shown, be patient and praise any attempts that show that your dog is getting the idea, even if he isn't successful at first. Keep the sessions very short – no more than three or four attempts each time. Play an easy game with your dog in between learning sessions too, so that he doesn't become frustrated if he's finding 'Catch the treat' difficult. Make sure that you also stand back as you teach him to keep his nose still. Dogs find anyone, even a well-loved owner, threatening if they get too close while looming over them, and your pet needs to be concentrating on what it is that you want him to do.

▲ ONE Your dog needs to learn to keep his nose steady first. Hold his nose very gently, while offering a treat as a lure in your other hand, and ask him to 'Stay'. If he can't keep still, he won't be able to balance the treat. Once he's learned this game you won't need to hold his nose, as your dog will understand that he needs to keep steady while you balance the treat.

▶ TWO When your dog is holding his nose steady, treat him, then, gently holding his muzzle, balance a small treat on top of his nose. (The dog in the pictures is a virtuoso and can toss quite large treats, but while your dog is learning, it's best to start with something small and light.) If he starts to move, tell him to 'Stay'. If he holds still for even a moment, praise him lavishly and reward him.

▼ **THREE** Now step back and make a sharp throwing gesture upwards with your hand. As your dog looks up at your hand – and dislodges the treat – give the command 'Catch'. Eventually your throwing action will encourage him to flip the treat.

▼ **FOUR** The reward at last! You've probably had to persevere with a few attempts when your dog simply slipped the treat from his nose into his mouth, and with a few others when he looked up at you and dislodged the treat accidentally. Finally, though, he's got it – and this is a trick that will win him lots of laughter and applause when he performs it with a bigger audience.

'Over' – Hurdling

If your dog is already eager to jump, hurdling won't take much teaching. A little routine in which she first leaps over the jump and then returns to wriggle under it is a bit more complicated. Keep the noises you make for over the jump and under the jump very different – a high-pitched 'Hup' together with an 'up' gesture of your hand will encourage her to jump over. You can make a jump – indoors or outdoors – with a broom handle placed across two cones of a suitable height. Make sure that the pole rolls off easily so that she won't hurt herself if she miscalculates on take-off.

▲ **ONE** Even if your dog jumps onto the couch or leaps low obstacles outdoors when she's playing, she may be a little more doubtful about jumping over a hurdle. Whether you set it up inside or outside, make sure that there's enough space for her to take a small run up to it, and start with it set very low – you can raise the bar when she's confident about tackling it. Ask her to sit on one side of the jump as you stand at the other, show her a treat as a lure, and lift it up and away, over the jump, saying 'Hup' as you do so.

▼ **TWO** She may jump right away. If not, try walking up to the jump with her and even taking a run and jumping yourself. Take it a few more times until she's jumping without hesitation. If the bar is very low, try raising it a little at a time. Now it's time for the limbo …

SAFETY
Jumping needs to be taken in careful stages. Elderly or arthritic dogs shouldn't be encouraged to jump too much, or, if they are really stiff, at all. If you're not sure whether a dog will be happy jumping, watch her everyday behaviour; if she jumps naturally while she's playing or jumps on or off furniture, teaching her to jump on demand will be fine.

And 'Under' – Limbo

Once your dog has learned to go over a jump, try showing him how to go under it. Just as a jump shouldn't be placed too high at first, so a limbo pole (which the jump now becomes) shouldn't be placed too low. When you're setting up, place the pole low enough for your dog to have to crouch a little, but not so low that she has to go straight into a flat-belly crawl. Practise a few times before trying to take it a little lower.

▼ ONE Place the pole at an appropriate height and show your dog a treat. Hold it low, with your hand very close to the ground. Your dog will stretch to reach it.

SAFETY Just as with jumping, crawling shouldn't be encouraged if your dog is old, stiff or has a bad back or hips. Use your judgement about whether this is a suitable game for him, but if you've decided to try it and he shows any discomfort at all, stop right away.

▶ TWO Pull the treat forwards slightly, so that it's a little further from your dog's nose. He'll naturally go down to stretch to reach it and so will begin to move under the pole. Keep it just out of his reach, saying 'Limbo' encouragingly as he moves.

▼ THREE As soon as he's successfully under the pole, praise your dog and give him a treat. Take two or three more practice runs, then, if he seems to be doing the limbo very easily, lower the pole a little. Don't lower it beyond the point at which he's in a flat crawl – that's low enough. Now try asking your dog alternately to jump over and limbo under the pole.

Laundry Service

Many dogs, particularly 'mouthy' breeds, such as spaniels and retrievers, love to carry soft fabric items in their mouths. If your dog already knows 'Take it', why not turn her natural inclination into a useful trick and teach her to collect the laundry for you? The hardest part may be getting your dog to let go of the things she's taken and to place them in the laundry basket; most dogs enjoy the collecting part the most, but will quickly learn to trade a treat for a sock or T-shirt.

▼ ONE Put a pile of laundry items on the floor on one side of the room and place the basket across the room from them. Pick up a sock and hand it to your dog, asking her to 'Take it'.

SAFETY Surprising numbers of dogs are taken to the vet each year to have socks or other small items of clothing surgically removed from their stomachs. Don't encourage your dog to 'mouth' on small items of laundry when you're not playing this game – if she loves to carry something soft around with her, buy her a custom-made, large, soft dog toy instead.

◀ **TWO** Have a treat ready and, as she takes the sock in her mouth, run over to the laundry basket with her (show her the treat to lure her if she needs encouragement).

▶ **THREE** When she's holding her laundry right over the basket, hold your hand out with the treat and, as she drops the sock into the basket, say 'Laundry service' and give her the treat. Run back to the laundry pile with her and choose another piece for her to collect. She'll quickly get the idea that she can swap laundry for a treat and will start to bring the pieces over for herself. As she gets familiar with the game, treat her for only every second or third piece of laundry. Eventually, just the 'Laundry service' cue will be enough to get her gathering up the laundry!

Freeze

Some children play a game in which a child tries to sneak up behind the 'person' as quietly as he or she can, and has to freeze in position when the person turns around. Well, this is a version for you and your pet to play. Not all dogs take to it, but even if you end up romping together as he fails to 'freeze' at the right moment, you'll both have a lot of fun. Ask a human friend to play alongside your dog to help him to get the idea of stopping and starting; he'll find it easier if he has someone creeping and freezing alongside him.

▼ ONE Have your friend and your dog stand a little distance from you, across the room (or the garden if you're playing outside). Turn your back to them. Ask your friend to move towards you very, very slowly and quietly. She can encourage your dog to move alongside her (a good cue for slow-and-quiet with dogs is a finger held to the lips) equally slowly and quietly. If she exaggerates how stealthily she's moving, he's likely to copy her.

▶ **TWO** When they're still some distance behind you, turn around slowly. Your friend will immediately 'freeze' in position, staying absolutely still. If your dog looks as though he's about to leap toward you, say 'Sta-a-a-ay', drawing out the word in a low, soothing voice. Then turn your back again.

▼ **THREE** Gesturing to your pet, your friend will begin to move forwards slowly again. This time, let her get all the way to you and 'catch' you before you turn around. Make a fuss of both dog and friend. Don't try more than two 'freezes' for the first few times you practise this game; your dog will probably get too excited and burst into activity if you ramp the tension too high. If he suddenly loses control and rushes over to you at the wrong moment, say 'Uh-uh' and ask him to go back in place.

Push the Ball

Some dogs are as fascinated by ball play as the most eager human football fan. If you have a dog who's an enthusiast, practise with her regularly to teach her how to push the ball with her nose, 'head' it when it's in the air, and run along, directing the ball with a mix of chasing and dribbling it, while maintaining perfect 'paw' control. If she can learn all this, you can play mixed dog/human ball games that will be enjoyable for both parties, and wonderful exercise for both you and your pet. Start by teaching her to push the ball.

SAFETY Choose the ball your dog plays with carefully. It should be a good weight and size – not too heavy for her to be able to push easily or 'head', and not so light that she simply picks it up rather than pushing it. A foam-filled, hard, pet ball of an appropriate size is a good choice; she won't deflate it if she accidentally sinks her teeth in.

▶ ONE Place the ball on the floor with a treat just underneath it. Call your dog over, and she'll push her nose under the ball to get at the treat. As she noses it and the ball moves, say 'Push'. Repeat two or three times, saying 'Push' every time she noses at the ball.

▶ **TWO** After a couple of sessions of practice, try asking her to 'Push' without placing a treat under the ball. For some dogs, the rolling ball is exciting enough without any inducements, but if she doesn't start to nose and push the ball right away, roll it towards her and ask her to 'Push' it back to you. Turn the interaction into a game and offer her a treat when she returns it to you.

▲ **THREE** As she gets used to pushing the ball around you can gently kick it towards her, skirt around her while she's dribbling it, and generally encourage her to join in with you playing with the ball rather than keeping it all to herself.

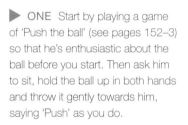

▶ ONE Start by playing a game of 'Push the ball' (see pages 152–3) so that he's enthusiastic about the ball before you start. Then ask him to sit, hold the ball up in both hands and throw it gently towards him, saying 'Push' as you do.

Head the Ball

If you've already taught your dog to push the ball, the next step is encouraging him to head it into the air. Make sure the ball you choose isn't too heavy or cumbersome – dogs can get excited in the middle of a game, so it's important that he can't hurt himself. Once he's learned to head the ball, you'll be able to teach him to score a goal or head it over a net, depending on your own favourite game.

▼ **TWO** He may immediately try to jump and push the ball. If he doesn't, have another try. Keep saying 'Push' whenever you throw, and as soon as he tries to nose it mid-air, praise him and give him a treat, even if he doesn't immediately succeed.

▶ **THREE** Don't expect your pet to learn to head the ball efficiently in just a couple of sessions. Practise little and often and alternate throwing and rolling the ball, so that he gets the opportunity both to head it and to dribble it. Wait until he's completely confident with 'heading' a thrown ball before you introduce other players (human or canine) to the game.

Agility
Challenge

A dog that just seems to fly through the air when she's playing ball with you, and is always looking eagerly to you for guidance and instruction, is likely to be a natural agility athlete. This section guides you through all the different activities in a professional agility circuit and looks at how you can set up your own garden version at home. If your pet is especially eager you may even find that you're doing timed rounds and joining a local agility class. Even dogs that aren't wild about the whole circuit usually enjoy one or two of the activities – if necessary, you can customise the course especially for your own pet.

Making a Garden Agility Course

Many dogs love energetic play with lots of jumping. If your dog is like this, and has also demonstrated that he can work things out for himself, you might want to consider building him his own agility course on which to practise. Take him to a local agility class for a few sessions, even if you're not interested in competing professionally; it will ensure you understand the proper use of the equipment and understand any safety issues. New equipment can be expensive, so look around for good second-hand items. If you decide to improvise, it's worth asking the advice of your agility class instructor, to make sure that the at-home entertainment centre you're giving your dog is safe, as well as fun.

▼ BELOW Jumping is a mainstay of agility trials. You can purchase professional jumps or improvise and build your own: just make sure they're not too high for your dog – he should be jumping no higher than his shoulder height.

SAFETY If you're setting up a garden agility course, make sure you've got enough space between obstacles. Jumps in particular need room for take off and landing – at least five strides for take off and four to recover.

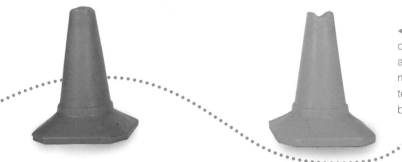

◀ LEFT Line up cones or other obstacles for your dog to weave in and out of. You can make this even more challenging for your dog by teaching him to dribble a ball between the obstacles.

▶ RIGHT A professional pause table is one metre square. It sits on a stand, which is adjusted to the height of the dog. In competitions, dogs have to pause on this table for five seconds before proceeding to the next obstacle. The table must be sturdy, with a non-slip surface.

▼ BELOW The overall length of a professional chute tunnel is between 4–5 m (13–16 ft). The entry and exit sections are made of rigid material so they don't collapse while the dog is barrelling through. A children's play tunnel is adequate for novices.

▶ **ONE** Your dog will be jumping on her own in no time, but first you have to show her what to do. Put her lead on, and jog up to and over the jump. At the same time, say 'Over'. Give her lots of praise and encouragement. You may find that you have to jump on your own the first few times, while she holds back.

Hurdles

These pictures will probably make you reconsider any preconceptions you may have had about which breeds enjoy agility. The little papillon shown here weighs just two kilos, but she can do a complete agility course with equipment scaled down for her size. Not all dogs are natural jumpers, though, so take it slowly and take your pet through the 'Over' exercise on pages 144–5 before you set up more than one jump; true agility will call for your dog to jump several times in a row, but start with one and, when she's happy and relaxed hurdling that, add another and then a third, leaving plenty of space between them for your dog to get ready for her second and third jumps. And if she seems daunted by the half-shoulder height recommended for the bar, start with a lower hurdle.

FIRST OF ALL

Measure the height of your dog's shoulder and divide this by half. This is how high you should build the jump when first teaching your dog. A broom handle balanced between two boxes or cones works well.

TWO Keep on jumping until she understands the game, then jump alongside her until she's obviously happy about it. Now, stop just before the jump and she'll jump it by herself. Gradually stop further away from the jump, while still giving the command 'Over'. Now it's time to introduce a second jump a good distance from the first and ask her to jump them in sequence.

SAFETY Make sure the jump you build is easily knocked over and is the correct height for your dog. This game is best played outdoors, but if you have plenty of space indoors then it can be a good game for rainy days: just make sure your dog is playing on a non-slip surface.

ONE Hold the hoop steady at floor level, or a little way off the ground. With your other hand, offer your dog a treat and then tell him to come 'Through'.

Hoopla

Jumping through a hoop is a natural progression from taking a hurdle. Your dog may hesitate a little more before jumping because he's not sure about the idea of jumping through an 'enclosed' space – even one enclosed by a barrier as insubstantial as a hoop. The lower and steadier you hold the hoop, the quicker your dog's confidence will build, and the easier he'll find the jump. If he continues to look uncertain about the idea, you can hop back and forth through the hoop yourself to give him some encouragement.

SAFETY Never ask your dog to jump higher than the level of his shoulder; you risk placing too much strain on his joints and muscles.

TWO Repeat the step, moving the hoop gradually up each time. Say 'Through' each time and soon your dog will be happily hopping through the hoop to get his treat.

▲ **THREE** When your dog is happy to hop through the hoop, raise it just – only just – to the level at which he'll have to jump. Then throw a treat to the other side and say 'Through'. He'll probably jump without thinking. If necessary, you can block off the sides of the hoop so that he can't walk around it!

▶ **FOUR** Once your dog is really accomplished at jumping through hoops, you can advance him to professional agility equipment, such as a tyre jump.

▶ ONE Start with a short tunnel at first and make sure your dog can see through it. Tell her to sit at one end of the tunnel, and kneel down at the other end so that she can see you. Encourage her through.

Tunnelling Out

Start this game with a short tunnel at first. If you're improvising, it can be as simple as an open-ended box, but make sure it's stable and won't move or collapse as your dog goes through. If she proves adept at this game, invest in a proper play tunnel; they're the cheapest part of an agility circuit. The most common difficulty when teaching a dog the tunnel game is having her double back when she's halfway through. Avoid this by standing at the tunnel's exit and calling her so that she heads towards your voice if she becomes uncertain.

◀ TWO As she exits the tunnel, praise her and give her a treat. Don't place treats in the tunnel itself, even at the beginning; you'll only be encouraging her to stop halfway through for a snack.

▼ THREE As soon as she's confident in the short tunnel, add a section (but just a short piece at a time). Run towards it with her, saying 'Tunnel'. When she's happily running through the tunnel at its full extent, add a curve in the middle to make the game a little more challenging.

▶ ONE Start the game by saying 'Ready, steady, GO!' in an excited voice, then start off around the course, running alongside your dog as fast as you can. Although he already knows the course, you may find that he skips one or two stages in his excitement and eagerness to keep up with you.

Race Against the Clock

Make sure that you and your dog are both in peak condition before you undertake to time yourselves around an agility circuit. Have a stopwatch and a friend ready, and warm up first with a brisk walk around the course. Then go around once, at a trot, checking to see that your dog can deal with all the obstacles. Finally, inspire him with an excited command and set off around the course together. Time yourselves first to get a best-out-of-three record, and then practise the aspects of the course that pose more difficulty to determine whether you can improve your time.

▲ TWO Do all the jumps yourself, don't just accompany your dog; that way, he'll understand that he shouldn't skip any of the stages. Keep the sessions short at first: once or twice around the course is plenty. You need to make sure he doesn't get bored with it!

◀ THREE After a few practices, he's ready to go solo. At first, you might have to ask a friend to hold him, then to release him as you race ahead over the obstacles so that he'll follow you, but he'll soon learn to do it on his own. Give the same command, 'Ready, steady, GO!', before racing against the clock, and always reward him even when he doesn't make his best time.

Group Agility

From holding a play date with your dog and a couple of her 'friends' to having them compete in your garden agility circuit is just a small step. As long as they're all in good physical condition (and, ideally, not too different in size and shape, otherwise you'll have to modify the course between rounds), they will often enjoy the opportunity to be put through their paces with other dogs around. If you find the thought of several dogs all getting excited together in your garden a bit too much to take, join a local agility class, where concerns of safety and organisation can be resolved for you.

AGILITY CLASSES

If you're attending a group class, don't forget to take lots of treats and some favourite toys. If you're going to be away for some time, take some food and water. And don't forget to bring spare bags to clean up after your dog if necessary.

▼ BELOW Don't worry if your dog gets a bit excited. For her an agility course with other dogs is like a wonderful party with entertainment as a bonus. Having to process all the new experiences, she may forget some things. Be patient with her and start again if she gets confused.

Going Professional

Have you ever wondered whether you and your dog's teamwork would be good enough to demonstrate at a competitive level? Professional agility as a sport is growing at an annual rate of 10 per cent a year – not bad when you consider the first agility trials were held in 1978 at Crufts in London. Dogs can start competing at about 18 months of age, and can keep going in special veteran classes until they're about 13 years old. If your agility training has been improving by leaps and bounds, begin by trying out your dog's and your own paces in a local agility contest, and find out how you do.

▲ ABOVE If you want to win, join your local agility club as soon as possible. This will accustom your dog to competitions and crowds, and you'll hear about all the trials in your local area.

TECHNIQUES & TRAINING

Make sure you keep up-to-date with the latest training methods and ideas if you're thinking of trying professional classes. Methods and ideas change faster than you might think!

▼ BELOW How well your dog performs at competitive level may largely depend on his breed. Large dogs, such as the Border collie have the right body conformation and temperament (as do Kelpies and German Shepherds). In the small dog classes, poodles and some breeds of terrier usually outperform the others.

Exercising
With Your Dog

If you're enthusiastic about keeping fit, this section offers you plenty of ideas for exercising alongside your dog. Whether you love hiking, running, cycling or team games the best, there's the possibility of bringing your canine companion along. With enough training time and encouragement, you can even teach your pet to play rounders or dog football. True, the games may not be quite as rigorous about the rules as the human versions, but you'll both still have plenty of fun.

Walking Together

The idea of leisurely country strolls with your pet may be one of the main reasons you got a dog in the first place. And no matter how many games you play with your dog, chances are that going walking will be the most time you spend together. Be aware of how fit your dog is: if he is elderly, injured, overweight or has breathing problems, make the walk a slow, gentle one. Even leisurely walking helps with fitness – both yours and your dog's – and having a dog can motivate you to get out whatever the weather, and at busy times when you'd probably otherwise find an excuse not to go out.

▶ RIGHT Keep your dog on a lead if you're in a park or public space. Alternate walking and jogging is enjoyable exercise for both of you.

▶ **RIGHT** Go to different locations, walk a range of routes and play a variety of games along the way. Walking is by far the best way to bond with your dog because it enables her to act in all the ways that come naturally.

SAFETY
Have your dog wear a collar with an ID tag that gives your name and address on one side and states that your dog is microchipped on the other (the latter fact may deter thieves). Get your dog microchipped: it's a minor procedure and an instant form of identification if he gets lost, and if somehow he also loses his collar and tag.

◀ **LEFT** For long walks, get yourself a pair of professionally fitted walking boots. Trainers won't do if you're scrambling up and down rough paths. Keep your dog on a lead, because you never know when you might have to pass through livestock or other dog hazards.

Running and Cycling

Running and cycling are both great ways to give a dog some challenging exercise beyond your usual gentle walk. A fit young dog will be able to keep up with you – and probably overtake you – on any running circuit, and many dogs enjoy running alongside cyclists as well. You'll need a few practice sessions to balance your pace with that of your dog's, particularly if she is running on a lead and you're cycling; you don't want to race your dog at a pace she can't keep up, nor to be pulled along by your dog at a pace too fast for you. When you've got the balance right, either activity is good for the pair of you, and your dog will start to look on with excitement as you don your fitness gear.

▼ BELOW Use your common sense. In any but the most remote situations keep your dog on a lead, and start gradually with any running or cycling programme.

SAFETY

Avoid the heat of the day; exercise early in the morning or during the evening. You may be able to 'handle' hot weather, but even fit dogs may not; they can't sweat and compensate for high temperatures. Make sure fresh water is available for your dog along the way. Be extra aware of your dog during harsh weather, both in the heat and the cold – hot pavements can burn pads; ice and melting salt can also hurt or irritate pads. Pay extra attention to how much you feed your dog – don't let her do vigorous exercise after a large meal. Allow at least two hours between her meal and the exercise. Don't ask a young dog or puppy to run far; it can damage their joint development. If you're not certain that your dog is up to running with you, have her checked over by your vet.

◀ LEFT If you're cycling with your dog running alongside you on a lead, you might consider buying a springer. This is a special lead device that attaches to your bike and prevents you from being pulled over by your dog.

Hiking and Camping

Don't leave your pet at home if you're a keen hiker or camper. Some hiking trails and campsites allow dogs to come along, and your dog will love a break in routine with the chance of plenty of exercise as much as you do. Remember to bring along sufficient food for the trip; if you're somewhere remote, you won't be able to replenish dog food supplies. Think about where your pet is going to sleep, too. It will probably be best to set him up with a blanket or a travel bed in a corner of your tent at night; you don't want him pursuing the local wildlife across unfamiliar terrain in the pitch dark, so it's better for him to be safe inside.

▶ RIGHT You'll both enjoy your time away more if you've prepared yourselves with some training. A walk around the block is not the same as a steep mountain trail, so make sure both of you are fit enough before taking on long hikes.

▼ BELOW A trip away can be good for downtime as well as activity. Most dogs are thrilled just to spend time with their owners in the great outdoors, away from the duller aspects of their normal routine.

▲ ABOVE A fit dog with no back problems is able to carry up to 30 per cent of his own body weight. A canine backpack is great for hiking. Get him used to the pack by loading it and putting it on at home, so he learns where his new shape will or will not fit.

LOCAL RULES

Make sure you check with the local authorities what regulations apply in the area you've chosen. Your dog may be allowed only if he's on a lead, and while that may be necessary for some dogs, it won't suit others.

SAFETY If your dog is microchipped or wearing suitable ID, this will help you if you become separated from him. Always clean up after your dog. If you're staying in one of the camping sites that allow dogs, it's only considerate to your fellow campers. Don't forget to pack antibiotic cream and some bandages in case of an accident, plus parasite control, if applicable.

Frisbee Fun

Your pet may already love Fetch games, but Frisbee calls for a whole new catching skill. Before you start play in earnest, throw or roll the frisbee along the ground, giving the command 'Get it' as you do so. Never throw it directly at your dog, but always at an angle and parallel to the ground instead. Once your dog is catching a frisbee on the ground and returning it, try throwing it into the air. Kneel down and gently toss the frisbee to your dog. If she misses catching it, pick it up. Don't give the frisbee to your dog until she catches it, otherwise she'll consider it more a passive toy than a form of exercise.

▼ TWO Start with at least two people as well as one dog! Gently throw the frisbee to the other human player. Your dog will quickly come between you and try to intercept the frisbee. Then you can do some throws specially for her.

▶ **THREE** Once your dog has the frisbee, tell her to 'Drop' it. As soon as she gets the idea that, just as with fetching a ball, every drop means another throw, she'll be keen to comply.

SAFETY Pick a fabric rather than a hard plastic frisbee; they're widely available and they won't hurt your dog's mouth. Don't play a frenetic, high-throwing game of Frisbee with an elderly or a very young dog; you may encourage her to overexert with a jump or twist too far. You can still play, but keep the game gentle.

▲ **ABOVE** Use a purpose-made Tug toy with knots on the ends. This is the simplest game of all: pick up the toy, let your dog make a grab for it, then simply tug on the other end. You'll almost certainly get tired of the game before your dog does!

▶ **RIGHT** Dogs will often naturally play 'Tug' with one another. It's a game that provokes a lot of play growling and 'yipping'. Just keep an eye out to see that no one dog is becoming too possessive of that toy, and let the dogs enjoy themselves.

Tug of War

Dogs play 'Tug' naturally: if you hang onto one end of something, such as a rope, even a very young puppy instinctively knows to grab the other end and start to pull it. Trainers used to recommend that owners didn't play 'Tug' with dogs; they felt it reinforced the dog's natural possessive instinct and encouraged aggression. That's now held to be rather an old-fashioned view; provided that your dog will drop a toy when you request it, 'Tug' is an activity that is safe and enjoyable for your dog. However, make sure he doesn't become too intently focused. The signs of this are easily recognised. His body will stretch out and go lower, he will aim a fixed stare at his opponent, and he will look 'frozen' in position; if this happens, break up the game and get your dog to re-focus on doing something else.

SAFETY

If your dog becomes over-obsessed with getting the Tug toy, stop the game and take the rope away to give him a chance to calm down. This game is not suitable for young puppies if they're losing their baby teeth: it's best for them to fall out naturally.

Doggy Volleyball

A dog that has learned to push a ball along the ground may be able to master the skill of heading it back to you with her nose. This is quite a difficult game for any dog to learn, so be patient and, as always, keep your training sessions fun and short. You stand a better chance of success if you've noticed that your dog has often tried to join in human ball games: she's already looking at you and trying to work out what to do. The hardest part for a dog is learning to 'head' the ball with her nose, when her natural impulse is to catch it in her mouth. To teach your dog volleyball you'll need a net (a children's tennis or badminton net is suitable) and a soft ball. The ball should not be too large, but big enough for her to be able to follow easily; a size just a little larger than a tennis ball is ideal.

▲ ONE Your dog needs to be familiar with the 'Push' command before you start (see pages 152–3). Get her to stand behind a low net; to begin with, this should be at a level no higher than her neck. Gently throw a small, soft ball just above her head and give the command 'Push'.

▶ TWO Your dog will need time to understand how to push the airborne ball with her nose, but she'll eventually make the connection. There are no short cuts in this game; your dog has to work out for herself that she's supposed to bounce the ball on her nose, not take it in her mouth. Don't worry about whether she gets it back over the net or not. In the early stages of learning, it's quite enough that she learn to 'head' the ball from her nose. Praise and treat her each time she manages it.

◄ THREE Patiently repeat the command 'Push' as you throw the ball. Once she's learned to bounce it on her nose, you can encourage her to aim it at you, back over the net.

► ONE Mark out your diamond in the park and divide into two teams. Your dog will always be on the fielding team. Give him a few human team mates (if possible) so he doesn't get too exhausted and they're there to help if he loses track of what he's supposed to do in the excitement of the game.

Doggy Rounders

What this game may lack in formal rounders skills and rules it will make up for in noise and fun. You may find it impossible to get your dog to follow the rules as the game hots up and he becomes more excited, but it's a great opportunity for him to take part in a team game. You need at least two people: one to bowl and one to bat – preferably more, plus any sort of enthusiastic dog. Your dog, naturally, is invariably with the fielding team. If he gets too overwrought to fetch the ball on his own, have a designated player run along with him.

IMPROVISE

Teams usually field at least four people for this game. If you don't have that many, you can try having just a batsman, a bowler and your dog as chief fielder, and enjoy a game in the garden rather than in the park.

SAFETY **Use a light plastic bat and a soft ball for this game, never real rounders equipment: it's far too heavy and dangerous for a game in which your dog is involved.**

◀ **TWO** As the batsman hits the ball and runs to first post, the first-post fielder should ask your dog to fetch the ball. Quickly! If your dog is a good sprinter, you might get the other team 'out' faster than you think. As more batsmen enter the game, the other post-fielders can call 'Fetch'.

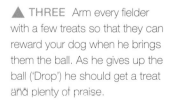

▲ **THREE** Arm every fielder with a few treats so that they can reward your dog when he brings them the ball. As he gives up the ball ('Drop') he should get a treat and plenty of praise.

Acknowledgements

They say you should never work with animals or children. The Ivy Press would like to thank Nick Ridley for his skill and good humour in photographing the dogs, and all at Hearing Dogs for Deaf People (www.hearingdogs.org.uk) for their help. Particular thanks go to Millie Smith for her forward planning, lateral thinking and superhuman patience during the photo sessions. We were grateful, too, to all the dog handlers and owners who helped and, of course, to all the dogs, who couldn't have been more fun to work with. They triumphantly disproved the truism about working with animals. The jury is still out on children.

Alice

Benni

Bertie

Brodick

Bruce

Busta

Byron

Cedar

Chutney

Fizz

Joey

JD

Juicie

Kai

Kia

Loki

Max

Mr. Flynn

Mole

Mojo

Odele

Samba

Scooby

Scout 1

Scout 2

Tawny

Teal

Tean

Tia

Toby

Tyke

Whisper

Index